P R A C T I C A L
STORAGE
SOLUTIONS

CONTENTS

EDITORIAL
Managing Editor: Sheridan Carter
Editorial Coordinator: Margaret Kelly
UK Editorial Consultants: How-To Publications

CONTRIBUTORS
Alison Magney (Tips); Andrew Kemp (The Cellar, pp. 76-78); Caroline Digiulio (Washday Blues, Bathrooms, Bedrooms); Christine Whiston (Getting Started, New Looks for Old); Dieter Mylius (Shelving It; Projects 3, 4, 6 and 10); Hugh Slatyer (Project Tool Kit; Home Office; In Easy Reach; Projects 7, 8 and 14; Skill Classes – pp. 7, 46, 53, 62); Jack Barrington (Skill Classes – pp. 25, 33); Mary Machen (Living Spaces, Multipurpose Areas, Storing Your Clothes); Michelle Gorry (In the Kitchen); Nadia Sbisa (Project 2); Robert Johnston (Tight Corners); Tonia Todman (Clever Ways to Recycle; Projects 5 and 13; Quick-fix Projects); Tony Todman (Project 9); Ursula Woodhouse (Outdoor Storage)

PHOTOGRAPHY
Features Editor: Sandra Hartley
Projects Editor: Tonia Todman

Photographers: Andrew Elton, Andrew Payne, David Young, Harm Mol, Vantuan (except where otherwise credited)

PRODUCTION
Tracey Burt
Chris Hatcher

ILLUSTRATIONS
Greg Gaul

COVER DESIGN
Frank Pithers

DESIGN AND PRODUCTION
MANAGER
Nadia Sbisa

PUBLISHER
Philippa Sandall

Published by J.B. Fairfax Press Pty Ltd
© J.B. Fairfax Press Pty Ltd 1990
This book is copyright. Apart from any fair dealing for the purpose of private study, research, criticism or review, as permitted under the Copyright Act, no part may be reproduced by any process without the written permission of the publisher. Enquiries should be made in writing to the publisher.
All care has been taken to ensure the accuracy of the information in this book but no responsibility is accepted for any errors or omissions.

PRACTICAL STORAGE SOLUTIONS
Includes Index
ISBN 1 86343 011 3

Formatted by J.B. Fairfax Press Pty Ltd
Output by Adtype, Sydney
Printed by Toppan Printing Co, Hong Kong

Distributed in the UK by
J.B. Fairfax Press Ltd
9 Trinity Centre, Park Farm Estate
Wellingborough, Northants UK
Tel: (0933) 402330
Fax: (0933) 402234

Distributed in Australia by
Newsagents Direct Distributors and
Storewide Magazine Distributors
150 Bourke Road, Alexandria
NSW 2015

Distributed Internationally by
T.B.Clarke (Overseas) Pty Ltd
80 McLachlan Avenue
Rushcutters Bay NSW 2011

Tel: (02) 360 7566
Fax: (02) 360 7445

New Zealand Agents
Medialine Holdings Ltd
P O Box 100 243
North Shore Mail Centre
Tel: (09) 443 0250
Fax: (09) 443 0249

*R*oll on the weekend! A time to stop, put your feet up, enjoy a drink, close your eyes and ... sink into a deep sleep? Certainly not! It's time to dream up your next home improvement project!

Let's face it – lack of storage can be a nightmare, especially with a growing family. Opening this book may well be your first constructive step towards a clutter-free life. Practical Storage Solutions *is full of space-saving and organisational ideas to help you out. Whether you are looking for home renovation ideas or design inspiration, there is something for everyone: feature stories; main projects, as well as quick-fix ones; skill classes; and tips, including 'green' ones.*

Every part of a house or apartment has different, pressing storage needs. Your individual needs will vary according to your lifestyle, the number of rooms you have, the amount of exterior space you can adapt, and the degree to which you are prepared to do a little lateral thinking!

All of the main projects in this book are rated according to degree of difficulty (see Key to Projects on page 4). Each project outlines what materials and special tools are required; the approximate amount of time the project should take to complete; step by step instructions; and lots of illustrations. Take your pick from the variety offered to suit your own situation.

The weekend is the natural time to undertake projects – after all, most of us only have the weekends to do work around the home. It's amazing what you can achieve, so why not give it a go? Spend a working weekend with Practical Storage Solutions.

KEY TO PROJECTS

 **SKILL CLASSES**

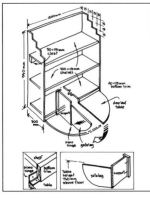

Project 1: Wall-mounted kitchen cabinet (page 17)

𝄃𝄃𝄃

Project 2: Storage cabinet (page 24)

𝄃

Project 3: Framing up an alcove (page 34)

𝄃𝄃

Project 4: Entertainment centre (page 38)

𝄃𝄃𝄃

Project 5: Fabric shelves (page 43)

𝄃𝄃

Project 6: Sewing centre (page 44)

𝄃𝄃𝄃

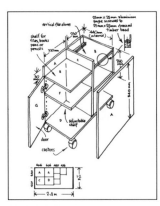

Project 7: Deskmate (page 51)

𝄃𝄃

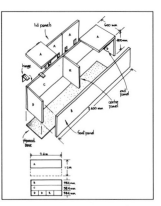

Project 8: Window storage box (page 52)

𝄃𝄃

Project 9: Under-the-bed storage drawer (page 57)

𝄃

Project 10: Laundry in a cupboard (page 60)

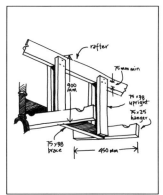

Project 11: Towel rack (page 64)

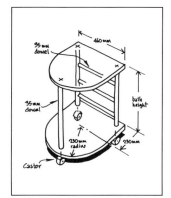

Project 12: Bathside trolley (page 65)

Project 13: Handbag tidy (page 68)

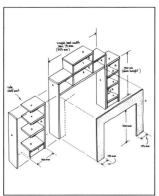

Project 14: Storage bed-end (page 71)

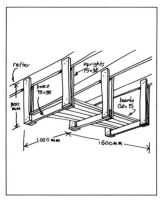

Project 15: Sturdy bicycle rack (page 75)

Project 16: Overhead storage rack (page 76)

Tool Kit

Most of the tools used in these do-it-yourself projects are fairly basic. The more specialised ones should only be bought as you need them. Remember, it pays to buy the best tools you can afford.

❏ Various tools are needed to accurately mark and measure your work. The most common and useful are a **rule**, a **steel tape measure**, a **marking or mortise gauge** (for the accurate marking of two parallel lines onto timber, such as for setting out the location and size for a mortise or tenon); a **try square** (used to make sure timber sections are at right angles to each other) and **combination square** (allows the stock to move along the blade, so that it can be used to mark different widths parallel to the side of a piece of timber), a **spirit level** (used to test the level and plumb of any piece of framework) and a **nail punch** and **centre punch** (to make starting points for nails and screws).

❏ To hold pieces of wood together tightly while adhesive sets and you put in nails and screws, you will need **sash cramps** (to span large pieces) and **G-clamps** (for general-purpose work). A **woodworking vice** is necessary for holding various pieces securely while being worked on.

❏ Some essential tools for joining and finishing include a **claw hammer** (to drive nails and withdraw them); a **cross-pein or pin hammer** (to drive small nails and panel pins – it has a tapered end called the pein, which is used for starting pins and tacks); an assortment of **screwdrivers** (for both slotted and crosshead screws); **pliers**; and an **adjustable spanner**. Also useful will be a **rubber or timber mallet** for striking wood chisels and tapping wood joints together; a set of **Allen keys** (for hardware installation); and a **filling knife** for wood filler.

❏ Saws are essential cutting tools. The most common types of handsaws are a **panel saw** (useful for light bench work and can also be used for light crosscutting and ripping or cutting along the grain); a **handsaw** or **crosscut saw** (can be used for ripsawing work as well as cutting across the grain); a **ripsaw** (used for cutting timber along the grain); **tenon saw** (used mainly for cutting tenon joints or for crosscutting small pieces of timber); and **coping saw** (used for cutting fine curves).

❏ Like saws, there are many different types of hand planes. The most common include a **jack plane** (used to do most of the rough planing work; the blade can then be set fine for finishing off); a **smoothing plane** (widely used for the final smoothing off before sanding timber); and a **block plane** (a handy small plane, which can be used with one hand so that the other hand can hold the timber).

❏ Chisels are also useful cutting tools. A good range would include **firmer chisels** (used for light mortising and trimming; socket chisels are a stronger type used for heavy work); **mortise chisels** (used for cutting out timber to make mortises; used with mallet); and **paring chisels** (used for shaping and trimming long flat surfaces where pressure is applied by hand, rather than by using a mallet).

❏ **Power tools** may be expensive but they *are* a good investment – paying off in time, labour and quality of craftsmanship. The **electric drill** is the most commonly used drill. It is available in a variety of types and speeds, including variable speed, and with or without a hammer action for drilling into masonry. For the handyperson, the best sized drill is one with a 10 mm chuck. This will allow for most drill bits that you will need. Other handy power tools include a **jigsaw** (for cutting round curves and in tight spots); a **circular saw** (for long, straight cuts); an **orbital sander** (for sanding); and a **router** (for making housing and rebate joints and for trimming edges).

❏ A **portable workbench** (Black & Decker) is one of those optional extras which make a lot of sense for some projects.

❏ An **oilstone** and **machine oil** are recommended for keeping tools well honed.

❏ A **protection set** is certainly worth the investment when it comes to safety. This includes a pair of goggles, a face mask and a set of ear defenders or muffs.

It is said that a good craftsman does not blame his tools – but it also pays to remember that good workmanship is not possible, in any material, without sharp and well-maintained tools.

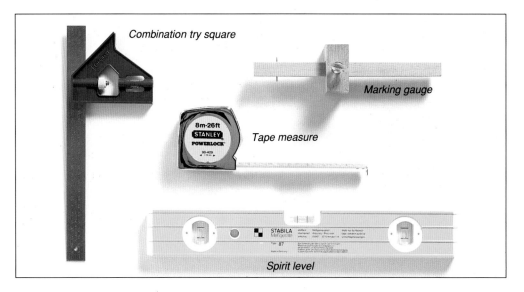

Combination try square

Marking gauge

Tape measure

Spirit level

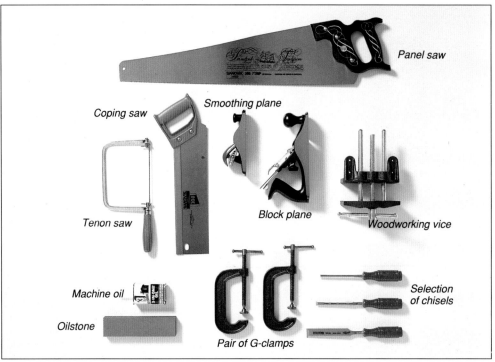

Panel saw

Coping saw

Smoothing plane

Tenon saw

Block plane

Woodworking vice

Machine oil

Oilstone

Pair of G-clamps

Selection of chisels

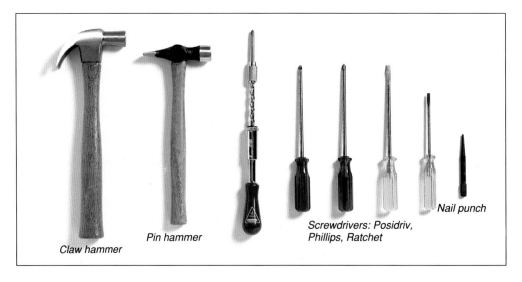

Claw hammer

Pin hammer

Screwdrivers: Posidriv, Phillips, Ratchet

Nail punch

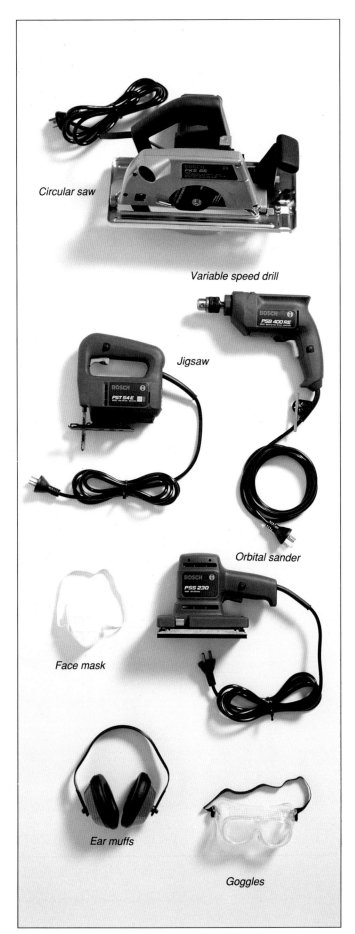

Circular saw

Variable speed drill

Jigsaw

Orbital sander

Face mask

Ear muffs

Goggles

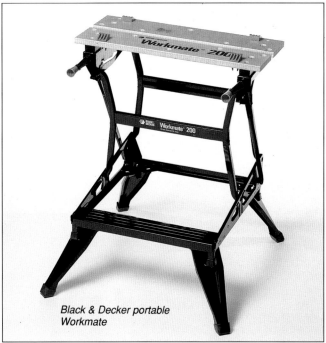

Black & Decker portable Workmate

 SKILL CLASS
Caring for your tools

CARE AND USE OF PLANES

❑ The first thing to remember is that you should never place a plane on its sole as this may damage the blade. Always lie the plane on its side.

❑ When using a plane, make sure the index finger is along the side of the blade, this gives better control. Most planing is done along the grain of the timber, that is, along its length. Set the blade very fine at first and then adjust it if you need to take more timber off.

❑ When starting to plane, place your weight on the front of the plane, and reverse the weight to the back at the end of the planing. Where possible, planing should extend from end to end of the timber so that the surface does not develop a concave shape.

Sharpening the blades

❑ The first stage is the grinding. This is done on a grinding wheel, using water on the wheel to keep the blade cool. The blade is ground to an angle of between 25° and 30°.

❑ The second stage is the honing, which is done on an oilstone with light, clean machine oil. The blade is honed to an angle of between 30° and 35°. When honing, you should move the blade in a figure of eight over the oilstone – this will prevent the stone from wearing down unevenly.

❑ After honing, the edge of the blade will have a slight burr on the back. Remove this by laying the blade flat on the stone and rubbing back and forth several times.

CARE OF SAWS

Saws should always be well maintained. Make sure that they are not rusty and that the handle is tightly screwed into the frame. A saw should always be hung up after use to maintain the setting and sharpness of the teeth. Protect the teeth by slipping over a piece of wood or hose split down the middle.

Saws need to be sharpened frequently. After three or four sharpenings the saw will need to be reset. Setting is the displacement of the teeth out from the main blade. Unless you are a regular handyperson with plenty of time, it is best to have your saws sharpened and set by a saw doctor.

When you can barely see into your wardrobe for clothes, your desk for paperwork, or your children's rooms for the layers of 'mess', you know you have a problem – mess has a mind of its own. It's time to roll up your sleeves and get started!

GETTING STARTED

Storage is often the last thing on the home-maker's list of priorities, and yet this practical and decorative aspect of home improvements is just as important as colour and furnishings to the way you use and enjoy your home.

All too often a simple task such as ironing a shirt can turn into a nightmare when the ironing board is stored at the rear of a cupboard cluttered with mops and pails, a carton of bottles put aside for recycling and the overflowing washing basket! Higgledy-piggledy storage may sound like fun, but the truth is, it is as inefficient as it is infuriating. Good storage is a question of balance – a way of dealing with (and finding) everything you use on a day-to-day basis (as well as the 101 items you use occasionally!).

Careful clutter notwithstanding, homes where there is a sense of order and a feeling of space are the easiest and most attractive to live in. It sounds simple, but careful planning and forethought will help you beat the mess and achieve this aim.

Assess the mess

Step number one is to take a pen, a piece of paper and a ruthless, assessing eye on a tour around the place. In each room, what is the nature of the storage problem? In the kitchen, are there too few cupboards? In the bedroom, is there too little hanging space? In the bathroom, are the towels taking over? In the children's room, are obsolete possessions still taking up valuable floor and wardrobe space? Is there a lot of 'dead' space around the place? For instance, are the beds high off the floor? This allows for under-bed storage or the construction of simple drawers.

Are your walls bereft of shelving, hooks and built-in cupboards? That's more dead space you can turn to your advantage. Have you thought of going up to the attic? Under the stairs? Excavating under the ground floor? Would renovations help? Additional rooms or an additional storey? Or would the mess just grow in proportion to the amount of space available to it? If the truthful answer to that last question is 'yes' then you know you need to take an even firmer grip on a deteriorating situation!

A plan of attack

Step number two is to sit down with the family, pen and paper in hand, and start making lists. Each family member should have something to contribute to the overall plan. Next, take those lists and massage and bully them into a single, workable concept. Sometimes it is useful to start with a very general list.

❑　Areas to be tackled
❑　Aspects to be retained
❑　Areas for renovation
❑　New possibilities for existing space

Swept-bare, possession-free living has romantic appeal, but the reality is that people like to surround themselves with all sorts of objects in order to live. Homes are the natural repository for these items.

IKEA

IKEA

Country Form

*Clockwise from top right:
A modern living room with freestanding units to suit; Sideboard for storage and display; Country-style kitchen; Wardrobe with stackable wire baskets; Family entertainment centre; Brightly coloured plastic storage boxes on castors – just keep stacking as you need more storage!*

Board games supplied by Toyworld

Stack 'N' Store, Woollen jumpers from Benetton

Country Form

- ❏ Budgetary allocations
- ❏ Design aspects
- ❏ Built-ins versus freestanding, modular or knockdown units
- ❏ Items requiring specialist storage

A checklist made up of questions can be very helpful.

- ❏ Is there a single room or area which could be made into a storage-only room?
- ❏ What extra space can you utilise for storage?
- ❏ Do certain items need to be stored in particular rooms?
- ❏ Is there storage space for sports and hobby equipment?
- ❏ Are there some items you need but can never find?
- ❏ Do you need somewhere

to put things you want to keep but not necessarily look at constantly, such as souvenirs from holidays, letters, and treasured collections?

- ❏ Are there some items you use more often in summer or in winter, so that you can organise storage on a seasonal basis?
- ❏ Do some of your possessions suffer from the way they are stored, such as:
  - tools that get rusty
  - clothes that get crumpled
  - fragile things that get broken
  - papers that get muddled?
- ❏ How much can you spend on storage?
- ❏ Will the storage facilities

you plan increase the value of your house or apartment?

The weeding-out process

It goes without saying that any genuine reappraisal of your storage needs ruthlessness. It makes no sense to invest in a fabulous new storage unit only to transfer years of accumulated bric-a-brac onto its shelves. The third step in the grand plan is a weeding-out process; going through those untidy drawers and bulging cupboards to 'rationalise' their contents.

Be constructive. Think about recycling out-of-date or ill-fitting shoes and clothes,

stacks of old magazines and newspapers. Consider a garage sale to rid yourself of saleable items and get rid of the rest.

SORT PILE: Things you want but have nowhere to keep. Put these things into bags or boxes and leave them for a while. The longer you leave the sort pile, the less you miss whatever is in it! Finally, your dread of sorting it will outweigh the dread of throwing it away. After taking out the things you really do need, it's two bags down and one box to go!

CHARITY PILE: Things that are still repairable or useful (to someone else), clothes and accessories – anything that can be used by someone or could raise money for a good cause.

JUNK PILE: Things that are broken, outdated, out of style, ugly, useless or mouldy – get rid of them, they are junk!

A room-by-room appraisal

Once you have a workable plan the next stage is to consider the specific requirements of each room. It goes without saying that certain parts of the home are natural storage areas, but also pay attention to the areas you may not have thought of, such as hallways, under the stairs, or up in the roof. Refer to the relevant sections in this book to help you with your room-by-room appraisal – you'll be amazed at just how simple a solution can be!

Winning the space race

Re-evaluating your existing space in terms of storage is imperative for the eventual

Tailor your storage units to suit a room's character and purpose

Country Form

Ornate freestanding wooden units with a limed finish

success of the storage system you choose. Try to think in terms of wall space. Objects at floor level, and thus in full view, take up more space and lead to a cluttered look. By moving items up off the floor and onto the walls, rooms will suddenly appear larger.

Streamlining is indeed the answer to most storage problems – the right storage will enable you to enjoy your possessions more and to indulge in the fine art of display. Remember that off-the-shelf units are customised by the addition of your own precious possessions, and this important designer aspect should be borne in mind throughout the various stages of planning.

A question of style

The possibilities for storage systems are as varied as those for every other type of household furnishing. Thus the final and arguably the most exciting part of your storage strategy is its overall design. Pay attention to:
❑ the age and architectural features of your home or apartment
❑ the style of existing furnishings
❑ personal design preferences
❑ the sorts of items to be stored/displayed
❑ future flexibility
❑ DIY potential

You can choose from a unit which will create visual impact in your home, or opt for something which will merge with the walls. Don't forget that large-scale storage units alter the proportions of a room and can be used to highlight or downplay architectural features such as windows or fireplaces.

Broadly speaking, the types of unit and system available fit into three designer categories: contemporary, classical and country – all of which have very specific characteristics. Contemporary design focuses on clean, uncluttered lines and makes use of materials such as tubular steel, glass, and lacquer/laminate finishes. Classical design features darker timbers and finishes, with traditional cabinet features and lines; whereas the country look features lighter timbers such as pine, slightly naive styling and a notable absence of fussy detail.

Again, you can create any of these looks by using a series of individual components. Buy ready-made units or, particularly in the case of kitchen storage, have something built to suit.

Don't overlook the importance of custom-

finishing your storage system. Colour – in the form of stains, stencils and painted finishes – can have a remarkable effect, and even simple additions such as new handles or door knobs can create just the effect you have been looking for.

A flexible future

The final point to take into consideration in your storage strategy is planning for the future. No matter how much storage you provide now, there will come a time in the future when it will need to be reviewed. This is where the wonderful flexibility offered by modular systems comes into its own, especially when planning for the needs of a growing family.

Take care not to lock yourself into a specialised system which can't be changed. Instead, try to aim for something which can be altered if necessary, added to or moved to another part of the house. Even custom-built units can be designed to include adjustable features with the potential for expansion.

If buying units for a child's room, think ahead to the time when a desk will be needed, and make sure there is room in the plan for such an addition. If installing a new kitchen, make provision for features such as an internal racking system which can be added as your budget allows.

Finally, remember that good storage will add enormously to the value of your home. A well-planned kitchen, effective wardrobes and cupboards in bedrooms, good use of space under the stairs and in hallways, are just the thing to strike the right chord with potential buyers, as well as simplifying life for you and your family.

With all of its pots, pans, bags of groceries and delicious comforting aromas, the kitchen is the heart of the home. But it does have a dual role to play: it has to be efficient yet comfortable and inviting.

IN THE KITCHEN

P lanning a kitchen may seem daunting at first, but most of the important decisions will be common-sense ones. Then you can spend time on the fun things like colour scheme and the overall 'look'.

Practical storage need not interfere with the visual aspect of your kitchen design and can often enhance many features. The kitchen is the main working area of your home and must be compatible with your lifestyle as well as easy to clean and maintain.

Whether your kitchen is modern, country style or industrial hi-tech in character, planning how it will work is the top priority. Kitchens tend to operate around three main activity centres: the stove, the sink and large storage areas, including the pantry and refrigerator. Ideally, the total distance between these areas should be between 3.5 m and 7 m for effective work efficiency (often referred to as the work triangle).

Work centres

❑ The main food preparation area is usually the worktop or bench space between the sink and the stove – this area should be large enough to prepare a meal on. If possible, the pantry or food storage area and any tall storage units should not interrupt the worktop space. Try to avoid gaps between appliances and units as this wastes space and makes cleaning difficult.

❑ The sink should be close to storage cupboards or shelves that house everyday crockery, cutlery, pots and glassware. Avoid plumbing a sink in a corner and allow space for a dishwasher and waste disposal unit if required. Consider draining baskets and a chopping board that fits over the sink if space is limited.

❑ Ovens and cooktops (hobs) are often separated today – both should be located near the sink so that steaming pots and pans can be carried easily. A centre island, which may house the cooktop (hob), can shorten the distance between major appliances and offer extra storage space. Avoid situating the cooktop (hob) in a corner – it should be well away from a wall cupboard or a window with curtains because of the fire danger. Large, deep pan drawers installed near the oven and cooktop (hob) are an advantage.

❑ Another cooking appliance that has become part of today's working kitchen is the microwave oven.

Consider positioning it for ease of use and allow clearance space for opening the oven door. Even if you don't have a microwave oven, it is wise to think about the space it *would* occupy (Who knows what you may receive for Christmas next year!)

Space to bake

For baking enthusiasts, here

Above top: Wall-mounted plate rack
Above: Pot drawers

Country Form

Styling: Michelle Gorry   Saucepans from Made Where

Clockwise from left: Pull-out pantry; Pale apricot kitchen; Appliance centre
Clockwise from right: Wine storage under breakfast bar; Stainless steel grid; Contemporary kitchen complete with shelf for microwave oven

Modern, country-style or industrial hi-tech kitchen? Planning how it will work is the top priority.

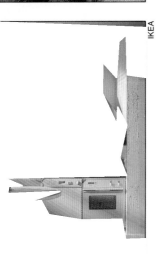

Made Where: Vasa Agencies; Accoutrement   Styling: Michelle Gorry

❏ A simple stand for a recipe book

❏ Measuring jugs, scales and an assortment of pans stacked neatly in overhead cupboards

❏ A stainless steel artist's ruler attached to a pull-out drawer for measuring pans and pastry

❏ A swing-out cupboard for drying home-made pastry

❏ A wall-mounted microwave oven on a swing-out bracket

❏ A telephone extension close by to avoid flour-coated telephone calls!

No excuses now if the cake doesn't rise!

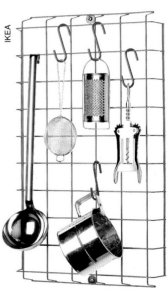

Utensils rack

Cutlery drawer

are some ideas for a wonderful kitchen area that tells the story of baking:

❏ A marble worktop for rolling dough and whisking egg whites

❏ Cupboards that open to reveal a pull-out filing device for baking trays and muffin pans: each tray stands

Zuhause; Vasa Agencies; Made Where; Accoutrement   Styling: Michelle Gorry

Carousel cupboard

vertically side by side (no more unstacking trays searching for the right size)

❏ Shallow drawers for cutters, rolling pins, piping bags and all manner of accoutrements

❏ An extension table or a fold-away shelf for an electric mixer, slightly lower than worktop height for easy viewing

Behind closed doors

Cupboard storage ideas are only as limited as your imagination.

❏ Glass doors can often be incorporated into cupboard design – these are generally at eye level to show off colour-coordinated china and glassware.

❏ Plastic-coated wire baskets are popular for storing numerous items from pots to vegetables.

❏ A tea-towel rack may be useful in a small narrow space.

❏ Storage units under the sink are useful for dishcloths, detergents, brushes and scourers. These units can be small baskets or swing-out compartments.

❏ Many kitchen designs now incorporate a fridge or a dishwasher behind a cupboard door – uniformity can easily be achieved with this clever design idea. When planning kitchen cupboard storage, consider items that are in constant use, those used from time to time and items that can be relegated to top cupboards or difficult corners. Make sure all your cupboards open in the most convenient way.

Drawing the line

Deep pan drawers are specially designed to hold saucepans, colanders and sieves, making them easily accessible. Very wide deep drawers can be useful for plastic containers. Shallow drawers are handy for cutlery and rolls of plastic wrap, aluminium foil and paper. Moulded plastic trays can assist with storing cutlery. Consider whether or not you require the space to store tea towels, tablecloths and napkins in the kitchen. Very small drawers can be used to store spices, balls of string, matches and piping tubes or other small items. Positioning

Country-style kitchen

Country Form

QUICK-FIX PROJECT
Storage racks on pantry doors
Why not make useful space of the inside of doors? It's easy to do with these purchased plastic shelves that screw onto the door.

Be sure to calculate the position of shelves so that they don't bump into existing shelves when the door is closed. Add another shelf under the sink for soap, brushes and cleansers.

drawers near the cooktop (hob) is often sensible for storing those indispensable items that you may need close at hand: thermometers, spatulas, ladles, tongs, timers, brushes, skewers, string and pot holders.

All drawers should run smoothly on runners.

Just hanging around

It is surprising what can be stored in overhead space if you are lacking floor or cupboard space. Plastic-coated or plated wire racks hung from the ceiling or the wall are useful for storage and display of pots and skillets. These should be hung within reach but above head height. A stainless steel wall rack can house cooking utensils and bottles of frequently used spices, oils and vinegars.

Generally this is situated near the cooktop (hob).

❏ Place hooks on the underside of shelves to hang cups, or hang a spice rack wherever it is most convenient. Tie up bunches of herbs and hang them from a shelf or curtain rail. A suspended plate rack is a solution for drainage and display. Decorative plates can be attractive when hung on a bare wall. Using a little imagination you can achieve very practical *and* attractive solutions.

Cost and practicality

Open shelving is one solution to low-cost storage. This need not lack style. Inexpensive glass jars containing ingredients can be very

The pantry

The old tradition of larder or pantry which predated refrigeration has not outlived its usefulness for food storage.

If your kitchen is large enough, a walk-in cupboard makes practical use of space. Heavy items can be stored on lower shelves or on the floor; regularly used items at eye level and items used occasionally on the top shelves. If you are fortunate enough, the room could be converted to a cool room for storage of fruit, vegetables and dairy products.

❏ A corner pantry is a clever way to utilise corner space, and carousel attachments and pull-out baskets allow easy access to deep corners. Door clearance is an important point to consider with cupboards and pantries. Varying shelf heights are sensible for ease of viewing items.

❏ Consider your regular shopping items and allow space for each item. Lower levels of the pantry can incorporate pull-out fittings, racks for spices, bottles and cans and trays for loose packets. Plastic storage bins can be fitted onto runners to utilise the top space of a deep cupboard. See-through glass or plastic jars or canisters of varying heights will keep food fresh and storage tidy. Wire baskets fitted into a drawer mechanism are an excellent idea for vegetable storage. Make use of wasted space on the back of pantry doors, with easily attached hooks, small storage baskets and racks.

A charming, old-fashioned pantry

Styling: Michelle Gorry

Country Form: Zuhause; Country Trader; Gallerie Nomad; Accoutrement; Appley Hoare Antiques

Vegetable basket

This kitchen features built-in white storage units and a free-standing rack for copper pots

attractive in line. Colour-coordinate your plates and glassware, and use shelving to display much loved items. Keep cookery books where they will be used. Anything that you may want to hide away can be curtained off or placed in inexpensive plastic tubs fixed on runners (colour-coordinated of course!).

QUICK-FIX PROJECT
Sideboard drawer divider
Are your heirlooms in a clutter? Consider dividing your sideboard drawer into made-to-measure sections to neatly contain its contents. First measure your drawer and cutlery, then draw up a plan of how best to divide up the drawer, allowing room for candles, bottle openers, carving knives and similar dining room needs. The sections are cut from plywood strips of a suitable height, then all are nailed or glued together to create a lift-in/lift-out drawer divider. Line the bottom of the drawer with a layer of fine batting or felt before fitting in the divider.

❑ A noticeboard is helpful to leave messages on and keep favourite recipes at hand.
❑ A magnetic strip can be attached quite simply to the wall near the cooktop (hob) for safe storage of knives.

Storing small appliances
How many times do you think about baking a cake or preparing fresh fruit juice, but the thought of rummaging in the back of a

top cupboard and lifting a heavy appliance down is enough to make you change your mind?
❑ A sensible idea to consider, if space permits, is an appliance cupboard. This is generally a narrow cupboard situated above the worktop, allowing you to use the appliances and store them at the correct height. A concertina door that folds as it opens is a space-saving option.
❑ Another option is to have

fitted a pull-out shelf that actually extends your worktop space for an electric mixer or food processor, or a fold-away mixer shelf that stows the mixer in the cupboard below the worktop when not in use. These shelves are often slightly lower than worktop height for easy viewing into a mixing bowl.

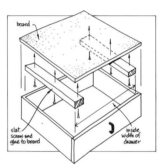

QUICK-FIX PROJECT
Kid's cooking drawer
Make a handy activity top to fit your kitchen drawers – your child will have a special worktop for painting or cutting out, or for assisting the master chef at those critical moments.

GREEN TIP
❑ **Pull-out bins encourage recycling of waste products like glass, metals, plastics and foodstuffs. Some units have a chute situated near the sink to place waste products into the bin, so the cupboard need only be opened to empty the bin.**
❑ **Recycle your glass jars as canisters: paint the lids a colour that coordinates with your kitchen.**

Wall-mounted kitchen cabinet

Keep your good china, glassware and other kitchenware close at hand in this clever kitchen cabinet.

STEP BY STEP

Except for the gateleg and the dropleaf, this cabinet is made out of softwood (pine).
Note: All joints to be drilled, glued and screwed throughout assembly.

1 Cutting out: Cut out all the components (sides, shelves, cleat, bottom trim, support flange, support, gateleg, dropleaf). Use a saw to cut the steps on shelf sides, and a jigsaw to cut the gateleg and table top to the radii shown.

2 Shelf unit: Start by fastening the batten/cleat to the under-side back edge of the top shelf. Saw 19 mm off the depth of the bottom shelf. Assemble the shelves and sides and complete with the bottom trim, flush with the bottom of the sides.

3 Gateleg: Screw through the back of the support flange into the back edge of the softwood support, using four screws evenly spaced. To allow the gateleg to swing freely, saw 12 mm off its top edge for all but the front 100 mm. Using the 400 mm length of piano hinge-ing, screw the gateleg to the front edge of the support (see illustration). Drill through the

support flange and screw the whole support structure to the wall with the table top at table height (see illustration detail).

4 Finishing off: Sit the shelv-ing unit on top of the gateleg and screw through the cleat to

wall-mount the unit. Screw through the bottom shelf into the top of the support. Use the 1100 mm length of piano hingeing to fix the dropleaf to the front trim (see detail). Finish with paint.

MATERIALS

ITEM	DIMENSIONS (mm)	QUANTITY
sides	1900 x 290 x 19 thick	2
shelves	3600 x 290 x 19 thick	3
batten/cleat	1200 x 90 x 19 thick	1
bottom trim	1200 x 40 x 19 thick	1
support flange	450 x 70 x 19 thick	1
support	450 x 240 x 19 thick	1
gateleg, high-density particle (chip) board	450 x 410 x 18 thick	1
dropleaf, high-density particle (chip) board	1200 x 600 x 18 thick	1
400 mm piano hingeing	400	
1100 mm piano hingeing	1100	
35 mm countersunk screws	35	
piano hinge screws		
PVA adhesive		
paint		

SPECIAL TOOLS
jigsaw

TIME
One weekend

SKILL CLASS
Using an electric drill

❏ When you are using an electric drill, make sure that you don't overload the motor by applying too much pressure.

❏ Always make sure that you are drilling square to the work surface. A simple way to do this is to align the drill bit with a try square placed on its edge. If

the hole has to be at right angles to the timber, such as for dowels, use a dowelling jig.

❏ The best method for absol-ute accuracy is to use a drill stand into which the drill is clamped – make sure that you get one which will take your drill.

The art of renovation is not limited to demolishing walls and raising the roof. Recycling should always be a priority and small-scale renovation projects offer great scope to the homemaker who likes to be creative.

NEW LOOKS FOR OLD

Many storage items lend themselves perfectly to renovation – so why not trade new looks for old?

When you're considering storage, don't make the mistake of thinking that the only way to improve the situation is to start again. Firstly, it is not always the most practical solution. Secondly, the constraints of budget rarely allow such luxury, and thirdly, in the interests of the planet, recycling should always be a priority.

A great many storage items have potentially exciting DIY possibilities. Take that battered tin trunk in the garage, for example, or that chest of drawers in the children's room that has seen better days. These are just some of the storage items lurking in your home which can easily and effectively be given a whole new lease of life.

In fact, once you start looking at old pieces of furniture you'll soon begin to realise that they simply don't make them like that any more! The high cost of materials and labour today has led to various manufacturing shortcuts and, despite the greater range offered, it has also led to the demise (in all but the most finely crafted furniture) of the cupboard that closes perfectly and the drawer that glides securely shut.

This is where recycling can be a real plus in so many ways.

Timber is a rapidly diminishing resource – why not help protect the world's dwindling forests by retaining existing timber pieces and revamping or renovating them? After all, one of the beauties of timber is its durability, and this alone is reason enough to roll up your sleeves and start being resourceful with what you already have.

Talking timber

The inherent beauty of timber, together with its practicality, has meant that it has always been our most basic building material. Throughout the years it has been fashioned into an enormous range of furniture, of which storage items are amongst the most common.

There are two ways to tackle the task of renovating timber storage pieces.
❑ Restoration – a process whereby the style of the piece is retained and its original finish restored.
❑ Revamping – whereby the original form of the item is retained but its finish and character is completely altered.

Why not renovate that old, wonderfully roomy wardrobe you inherited from your great aunt?

It may not fit in with the rest of your furnishings yet – but it will with a little work and decorating flair.

Workbench from Country Form

Above: A revamped industrial workbench used for storage and display
Right: This old, galvanised tin has been painted in an interesting way to give it a new lease of life

Restoring an object or an item of furniture is a classic form of recycling – and you can be experimental and creative at the same time. Why not stand back and reconsider your junk? You could be in for a pleasant surprise.

Left: This kitchen sideboard is excellent for storage and display of crockery and lends a rustic character to the room
Below: This second-hand shop bargain was restored by stripping back and staining (see Project 2 on page 24)

Kitchen safe from Country Form

Country Form

Tin from Country Form

Clockwise from left:
A wooden cabinet restored to make the most of the woodgrain and positioned in the room to contrast with stained timber wall panelling; Old cane suitcases revived by spray-painting; An old kitchen safe as is, used as a cabinet for storing crockery

Furniture from Country Form

This timber chest has been painted green over the original paint and then rubbed back

Restoration

The revival of interest in old-style, antique or rustic 'cottage' furniture has meant that pieces such as country-style dressers and chests of drawers are becoming harder and harder to find. All the more reason then to 'rescue' one you stumble across, tucked away in a second-hand store (or your garage!).

There are two ways of tackling the restoration of timber furniture: chemical stripping and sanding.

Chemical stripping

Because of the popularity of styles characterised by their rough-hewn or hand-crafted appearance, it is no longer necessary to achieve a flawless finish. This has made it a great deal easier for the DIY enthusiast. If your preference still tends towards a surface free of any traces of old paint, varnishes and stains, you may have to consider having the piece professionally stripped. This is the most effective way of getting back to the raw timber beneath; it is also the most practical way of dealing with larger pieces.

An acid bath is the most common method used and the item to be stripped is literally dipped into the stripping solution to remove accumulated surface coatings.

If you are working with a small item such as a timber chest, it is possible to strip the timber by hand. There are many commercial preparations available for these small-scale projects, but remember it is still a time-consuming and rather messy task. For this reason alone, it is important that you have some idea of the timber underneath before you go to the trouble of stripping it back. The craftsmanship and/or detailing of the piece itself will very often give you a clue. If you are in any doubt, test-sample a small area at the back or side before you commence work. The experts do not recommend that either timber veneers or particle (chip) board items be caustic-stripped.

GREEN TIP

The safest and cheapest way of stripping paint is dry scraping, but it is slow work and only suitable for small areas. Use a two-bladed scraper, with a serrated and a plain blade, to speed things up.
❏ Score the surface lightly using the blade with the serrated edge.
❏ Remove the paint with the plain edge. Be careful not to scratch or score the wood.

Sanding

Sanding is the other method used to remove accumulated layers on timber surfaces. It is hard work but rewarding, and the effects will be most gratifying.

Start with a coarse grade of sandpaper graduating to finer grains as the sanding proceeds. Once the timber has been reduced to its (nearly) original state, the process of filling and smoothing must be tackled. Whatever finish you are to apply, be it natural or a painted one, it is important that the surface you are working on is as clean and free of imperfections as possible. Paint, wax or sealants will not adhere to dusty, damp or grimy surfaces.

SKILL CLASS
Paint stripping

It is not necessary to strip paint just because the surface has been painted a number of times. A good number of coats will provide more protection. On the other hand, badly blistered or peeling paint will need to be stripped. If this is confined to isolated areas, strip the faulty area only.
❏ Scraping paint is best done with a scraper used in conjunction with heat, either from a blowlamp or electric heat gun or stripper (both of which can be hired). Play the heat source back and forward across the surface so that the paint is melted without damaging the timber surface.
❏ Chemical paint stripping has a number of advantages. There is no likelihood of damaging the timber, particularly important if you intend to stain it afterwards. Chemical stripping has the added advantage that you can work close to glass panels, such as those in old doors.

If you are going to strip paint from metal, make sure the stripper is suitable first, as some chemicals may etch the surface of the metal. Always read the information on the tin before buying.

Apply the stripper and wait for the chemical action to take place. Remove the old paint with a scraper for wide surfaces and a shave hook for mouldings.

After stripping, clean down the surface with turpentine (white spirit) or white vinegar to neutralise any chemical residue.

If you are looking for a natural finish there are a number of options available. Before deciding, give some thought to where the piece will go. A soft beeswax finish, for example, is inappropriate for a child's room where it will be subjected to harsh wear and tear and possible spills. The glow of a beeswax finish is better suited to a storage item which will be on display perhaps in the living room or hallway.

For a harder wearing natural-look finish, there are various other options available. Restored timbers can be oiled, varnished or finished with one of the many commercially available timber sealants. You can opt for low or high sheen, remembering that a low-sheen finish tends to show less marks. Most major manufacturers of timber finishes also offer brochures with detailed advice on their products. Make sure you are fully informed about a product before using it.

Revamping

A smooth timber surface provides the ultimate bare canvas for a whole range of exciting decorative painted finishes which can completely alter the character of a piece and even totally disguise the fact that it is made of timber at all. These finishes are ideal for lower quality timbers and timber veneers, and old pieces which have been sanded back to the bare wood.

Painted finishes

Painted finishes are currently enjoying a renewed popularity. A standard painted finish is one where colour is applied to a surface to either create contrast or to help an item blend with the existing surroundings. A decorative painted finish, on the other hand, can achieve an extraordinary range of

special effects, adding another dimension to painted surfaces. Some even go as far as to deceive the eye altogether.

Apart from their good looks, the other appeal of painted finishes is that anyone can master them. The techniques are quite straightforward. Have all the necessary materials to hand and make sure you have practised the chosen technique on a piece of card or board before beginning work.

The decorative painted techniques you will find useful for revamping include dragging, rag-rolling, sponging and stippling.

Inside out

Whether you are restoring or revamping, don't forget the inside of that wardrobe or chest. Renovation applies equally to the interior of storage units, since very often existing space is ill-used or wasted altogether.

Built-in units are the prime candidates for the wardrobe crush, and the easiest way to resolve this is to revamp the interior with an internal racking system of some kind. The most effective of these are the wire basket systems which are available in various sizes and stack into a lightweight frame which is fitted into your existing cupboards or wardrobes. By flat-stacking items such as shoes, jumpers, underwear or towels, you'll free up space for hanging clothes or for storing taller items.

The same principle applies to your kitchen cabinets. You might not be in the market for a new kitchen, but by revamping the interior space you already have, you can sometimes double your existing storage potential. Look for units to make drawers more efficient, corner units for those hard-to-get-at and all too often

wasted areas, and racks to hang brooms and mops, thus freeing floor space in larger cupboards.

Simple additions too can make a world of difference. Adjustable shelving, for example. A cavernous cupboard will, in fact, contain less than a smaller, efficiently outfitted one. All you need is one of the many racking systems available, or a set of additional shelves precut to the desired size. This is an ideal weekend project for the home handyperson.

Specialist storage shops and kitchen specialists will provide a plethora of ideas and inspiration as will commercial storage outlets. The systems designed for use in offices, factories and shops can work just as effectively in your home and are very adaptable.

GREEN TIP
Cleaning metal the friendly way:
Copper – Rub with vinegar using a soft cloth. Polish with a dry cloth.
Chrome – Polish with cider vinegar, or dip a dry cloth in ordinary flour and wipe over.
Brass – Shine brass using a paste of vinegar mixed with bicarbonate of soda, or Worcestershire sauce.
Pewter – Polish with the outer leaves of a cabbage and then buff with a soft cloth.

A long narrow cupboard with a blue duck stencil pattern on the door

Cupboard from Country Form

Rag rolling

This is considered a basic technique. The effect is achieved by lifting some of the topcoat of colour from the basecoat (usually a lighter shade such as cream or a pastel) with a scrunched-up rag which has been soaked in solvent. A random textured effect is created as the lighter basecoat is revealed beneath the darker topcoat.

❑ Working on a clean, dry surface, apply the basecoat and allow it to dry. Apply the topcoat sparingly. It can be thinned to achieve the desired translucence.

❑ Using the solvent-dipped rag scrunched into a sausage shape, simply roll lightly across the freshly painted surface, removing as much of the topcoat as you can to create the desired effect. The action is rather like rolling pastry with a rolling pin.

❑ Work on a small area at a time and discard the rag for a fresh piece once it has become too loaded with paint. Work in strips for ease of application and uniformity.

❑ When dry, apply a coat of clear polyurethane for protection.

Dragging

This method is similar to that for rag rolling except that a wide brush is the tool used and this is literally dragged vertically over a wash of colour. The effect achieved is one of even texture. It is important to work with a topcoat that has been thinned down to the correct consistency. Oil-based paints are ideal because they don't dry as quickly and will not run.

❑ The project is best tackled by two people – one applying the strip of colour wash, the other dragging the brush down the wet surface.

❑ Work around vertical lines. Begin dragging where a natural vertical exists, for example, on a drawer or cupboard door.

❑ Clean the brush on a rag after every few dragging strokes

Sponging

and clean excess paint off the surface before it has a chance to accumulate and dry.

❑ A coat of clear polyurethane should be added for protection once the surface is completely dry.

Sponging and stippling

The techniques used for these effects are similar – one uses a sponge, the other a stiff, circular stippling brush – but the results are quite different. Sponging a colour onto a washed surface achieves a soft, country-style look, whereas stippling gives a more controlled effect. Both are ideal for medium-sized pieces such as a timber chest, a bedside table or corner cabinet. Polyurethane can be used to protect the finish.

Special effects

A close relation to painted finishes are the special effects which can be achieved with paint. Some of the most popular include stencilling, decoupage and trompe l'oeil finishes such as marbling. A little more

precision is required with these techniques but the results can be sensational.

The sorts of items suitable for stencilling or some form of faux finish include smaller chests of drawers, timber trunks or chests, bedside cabinets, spice racks and so on. A variety of surfaces can be worked on: prepared timber, old or new, is ideal but metal and even glass can also be decorated this way.

Stencilling

Stencils are most often applied as a border and provide an ideal embellishment for ordinary storage items. You can customise a chest of drawers, for example, by adding a simple floral or geometric motif to the top and bottom of each drawer, or to the corners of cupboards on a bedside cabinet.

❑ When applying stencils, which you can either create yourself or buy ready-made in kit form, it is important to fix the stencil in place – masking tape is ideal – and apply the paint carefully to prevent it running underneath. The paint

Stencilling

needs to be just the right consistency. It is wise to experiment on a piece of old timber or card first.

❑ Apply the paint with a circular stencil brush, using a dabbing motion and working from the sides to the centre of the stencil. Make sure all gaps are filled with colour, leave to dry for a few minutes then carefully remove.

❑ Wipe any excess paint from the stencil before applying to the next area.

❑ If you plan to work with more than one colour, complete the first colour before adding the second or third.

If you are anxious to practise the technique before tackling a large item, try your hand on something small and easy to handle such as an old cutlery storage box, which is practical as well as pretty.

Decoupage

This is a delightful effect and one ideally suited to old travelling trunks, even old suitcases, toy boxes and so on. It's fun and easy to do and the results are very individual.

The technique involves cutting out motifs and gluing them to a surface to form either a pattern or picture. You can use just about any image that takes your fancy. A collection of old birthday cards, for example, would be a superb way to cheer up a toy box. You can opt for an all-over effect, or create a pattern inside the lid of a chest or just on the corners. Make sure the working surface is clean and dry before fixing the images with a strong paper glue or woodworking adhesive. The more coats the better, as the cut-outs then disappear into the thickness of the varnish and give a smooth surface (lightly sand between each coat).

Marbling

This is the method whereby timber (usually) is made to look like marble. The effects can be quite dramatic and wonderfully deceiving. It is an excellent device for an otherwise plain

built-in. As with all these techniques it is important to practise first so that you are reasonably familiar with the method before commencing work on a piece of furniture.

❑ To achieve a marbled effect, apply a series of vein-type patterns in dark shades over a light gloss basecoat to resemble the veiny effect of marble. Use a feather to create a marbled effect: apply vein-type lines with a deliberate wriggly movement so that the edges are slightly blurred. Use the lighter contrasting shade for larger veins, the darker for the smaller ones. You can also gently sponge vein lines to further soften the effect. Highlights can be added later.

GREEN TIP
❑ **Wrap containers of leftover paint and turpentine (white spirit) before putting them in your bin.**
❑ **Choose water-based paints over oil-based whenever possible.**
❑ **Clean your brushes away from drains.**

QUICK-FIX PROJECT
Decoupage jewellery box
This old cash box was a junkshop find. While it was solid and needed only minor repairs, the hinges and metal fittings had to be replaced. The metal pieces were removed first to provide a smooth surface to treat. To achieve this montage effect on a similar find, sand the wood back well, and fill any cracks and dents with wood filler. Stain or paint box if desired. Seal box with one coat of polyurethane, allow to dry then lightly sand. Cut out motifs from paper, and apply to box with woodworking adhesive. Cover motifs and box with another coat of polyurethane, then sand again. Give the box another five coats, sanding back between each coat. When completely dry, replace the hinges and handles with those of your choice, adding corner protectors if desired. Line the box with velvet panels and braid to complete.

Right: A stencilled tin chest

Stencilled bread bin and wall border

Storage cabinet

French polishing is a skilled craft but, using proprietary solutions, it can be tackled by anyone with patience for that special piece of furniture that is beau but not faux.

STEP BY STEP

1 Remove broken latch and strip wood veneer off top panels.

2 Rub down timber with methylated spirits using steel wool to remove lacquer.

3 Sand all areas with medium-grade paper to remove minor blemishes. (Note that we wanted to retain an antique quality so not all marks were removed.)

4 Wipe down all surfaces with a damp cloth to remove any dust and loose particles.

Above left: Stripping wood veneer off top panel
Left: Using steel wool and methylated spirits to remove lacquer

5 Cut new wood veneer panels to size and iron onto surface or glue plain veneer panels with thixotropic contact adhesive (this will allow slight repositioning). Allow panels to adhere.

6 Apply stain to all areas of timber and new wood veneer and allow to dry overnight.

7 Prepare polishing pad by taking a wad of cotton wool (the size of an egg) and fitting it snugly into a piece of cloth. Create an egg-like shape and twist cloth tightly behind pad.

8 Dip cotton pad into proprietary French polish solution or shellac mixture and apply sparingly in long, sweeping movements. Cover entire area and allow to dry for at least ten minutes before applying second coat. As many coats as desired can be applied, depending upon the gloss finish preferred.

9 Select and attach new latch for cabinet door.

Above: Sanding down
Below: Wiping down with a damp cloth

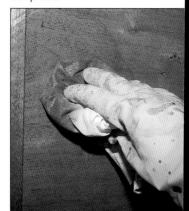

MATERIALS

ITEM	QUANTITY
sandpaper	4 sheets
steel wool	1 packet
methylated spirits	1 can
stain	1 bottle
cotton wool (medicinal type)	20 cm x 20 cm square
lint-free cloth	1 piece
iron-on wood veneer or plain veneer panels and thixotropic contact adhesive to glue	1 packet
proprietary French polish or shellac mixture (part shellac, part methylated spirits)	
new latch	

SPECIAL TOOLS
paint scraper
hammer and chisel (for hard-to-get-at places)

TIME
One weekend

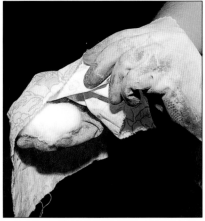
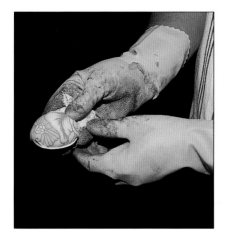

Preparing the polishing pad

Attaching the new latch

SKILL CLASS
Plugging a wall

To fix brackets or other items to a brick or masonry wall it is necessary to drill and plug the wall. Types of plugs are shown.

Plastic plugs are preferable for a screw fixing and a wooden plug 10 mm to 12 mm in diameter is suitable when a nail fixing is adopted. To select a plastic plug, first determine the gauge of the screw to be used and select a suitable one from the range of plugs usually available in hardware stores. The length of the screw should then be equal to the length of the plug plus the thickness of the item to be fixed.

To drill the wall you will require an electric drill, preferably a hammer drill, and a masonry bit the correct size to suit the plug. Mark the position of the plug on the wall with a cross, this will allow you to note if the hole drifts off-centre. Place a mark on the masonry bit to indicate the depth of the hole equal to the length of the plug, plus about 10 mm.

Hold the drilling machine square to the face of the wall and commence drilling, first pressing lightly until the hole is seen to be started in the correct position. Press firmly on the drill to keep it cutting and not just rubbing in the hole (this will blunt the drill), and continue until the required depth is reached. Clear the waste dust from the hole and drive the plug into the hole until it is flush with the surface.

Hold the item to be fixed in position, enter the screw into the plug and tighten securely. Note: When fixing into soft plastered walls make sure that the plug is long enough to penetrate sufficiently into the firm masonry below. Most importantly, beware of drilling into a water pipe or electric cable that could be bedded just below the surface.

PLASTIC PLUG

PLASTIC PLUG

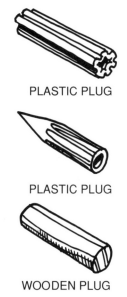

WOODEN PLUG

TIPSTRIP

TOOL HIRE CHECKLIST
❑ Ensure that the tool is demonstrated to you and that you are familiar with its operation and safety.
❑ Be certain that the equipment you choose is right for the job. Ask for advice if you are not sure.
❑ Read and understand the hire contract. The major companies offer an insurance cover against damage. This is economical and worth considering if you are doing a heavy job with expensive equipment.
❑ Be sure to include any necessary safety equipment when you hire. Gloves, goggles and so on are often essential when using power equipment.
❑ Don't be tempted to rush a job, particularly if you are using unfamiliar and potentially dangerous equipment. It's far better to extend the hire period.

Clever ways to recycle

*Just because a piece of furniture looks old and shabby, it does
not mean it has to stay this way or be discarded.*

Old or antique furniture was usually made from quality timber and had a craftsman-like finish. Furniture makers of yesteryear had time to create well-designed pieces that were both functional and very stylish. These qualities alone make furniture recycling a worthwhile exercise.

Modern lifestyles and changing needs also demand a practical and often ingenious approach to home furnishing, especially where storage is concerned. When you are on a shoestring budget and have minimal or odd spaces to play with, you need to carefully assess how and where a piece of furniture will fit in. So find yourself some wonderful, old or down-at-heel treasure and start by analysing its potential.

Does it have 'good bones'? Look beyond the shabby outward appearance of an object for fresh new refurbishing ideas – for example, the basic bookcase. It may be covered with peeling paint, look uninteresting and, as it stands, certainly wouldn't fit in with a fresh, bright furnishing look. However, once it has been repaired, stripped and perhaps stained or repainted, there are many decorative and practical ways of using it.

You could fix it to a wall above floor level and make a set of feature shelves; use it as a bedhead or a room divider; fit it into or in front of a no-longer-used doorway to display a treasured collection; place it in the garage for extra tool storage; cut it into two lower units and seal it with paint to make an accessible pot-plant stand; or stand it in a hanging-only cupboard as storage for folded clothes and shoes. Your once-shabby bookcase can be transformed in even more subtle ways by covering it completely with wallpaper or fabric to blend in with the rest

of your decor. The list goes on – and this was only a humble bookcase!

Once you enter into the spirit of searching for unwanted treasures, you will begin to see possibilities in just about any piece of furniture. But beware, it's important to recognise the strengths and weaknesses of your 'find'.

Thinking about buying and refurbishing an old cupboard? There are many real advantages in doing-up an old cupboard: good-quality timber and workmanship, spacious deep drawers and generous hanging capacity, for example. There are, alas, some potential drawbacks.

❏ Is the timber used heavily lacquered? This may be a real problem to strip and restain; in this case you may be forced to paint over the lacquer.

❏ Is it solid and free of insect attack? Look for tell-tale small holes and piles of sawdust. Professional fumigation may be required, or treatment with woodworm fluid and polish to restore the surface.

❏ Does it have door hinges and locks? These can be replaced but often not cheaply. Quality brass fittings can be expensive at retail outlets, so shop around. Brass restoration experts often have oddments available, and are well worth visiting.

❏ Do the drawers run smoothly? You may need to

QUICK-FIX PROJECT
Tin chest
A rummage in the garden shed revealed this charming, well-shaped old tin trunk patiently awaiting its chance for a new life. It was not rusty and only needed a sanding back to prepare it for a coat of paint. Undercoat and paint suitable for painting metal were used, and the pattern was created using a commercial stencil and spray paints. Most commercial stencils have simple-to-follow instructions on the packaging. When using spray paints to stencil, instead of brushes, use a piece of cardboard as a screen to prevent excess spray paint escaping and drifting, to land where it's not needed!

replace the drawer runners or use sandpaper to smooth off damp-swollen timber.

❏ Can you get the cupboard through the door when moving it to its new address? If the tape measure says this is not to be, is it possible to unscrew parts of the cupboard and reassemble it once moved?

Visit auctions, fairs, church bazaars and garage sales. Check the newspaper often for auctions of office furniture (you'll be surprised by the variety *and*

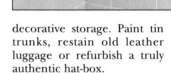

GREEN TIP

Here are just a few suggestions for ways you can extend the life of an item.
❏ **Start an 'ecology store' in your home. Store reusable items such as paper, string, boxes, cartons, plastic containers, ribbons, wool and fabrics to provide materials as the need arises. Set aside a drawer or cupboard for this purpose and encourage the whole family to use it.**
❏ **Re-use jam jars – wash and use again for food storage, keeping nails in, pencil holders and for the children to use in all sorts of ways (to hold water and paintbrushes, for example).**
❏ **Decorate old glass bottles and jars by painting them. This was all the rage in Victorian times for keeping lavender water, bath salts and other toiletries in. Store herbed oils and vinegars in bottles. Seal with corks.**
❏ **Re-use plastic bags for wrapping sandwiches, storing and freezing foods and keeping stockings tidy and snag-free.**
❏ **Start a household 'rag-bag' for storing all your clean fabric discards – dressmaking leftovers, torn sheet remnants, and worn out T-shirts. These can be used for so many different jobs – applying waxes and cleaners, washing windows, cleaning the car, mopping up stains or lining a box or basket for a new puppy or kitten.**

the bargains!). Two second-hand identical filing cabinets, perhaps repainted then set apart by about 1.5 m with a wide softwood table top resting across the tops makes a fine desk. If no old table top is available, consider buying a new one from contemporary knockdown furniture suppliers.

Remember that storage opportunities often present themselves in obscure and unpredictable ways. To help you with your treasure hunt, consider how different pieces of furniture can be adapted.

❏ Tables may have legs shortened to become casual occasional tables. They are perfect for stencilling or covering with fabric, and are a natural for a simple paint-over.

❏ Strongly woven baskets provide all sorts of storage possibilities: paint them, line them with fabric, stack lidded baskets, or use them in rows on open shelves for kitchen storage. Flat baskets with rims can become excellent trays. Old cane laundry baskets make ideal toy storage and can easily become a decorative feature when cleverly coloured. A deep, strongly woven basket with handles can be both stylish and practical when filled with wood ready for an open fire. Leave it outside under shelter for wood storage all year round, and carry it in when the weather sends smoke signals.

❏ Old luggage can provide

QUICK-FIX PROJECT
Creative wine storage
Out-of-use fireplaces can provide an ideal place for wine storage. Fireplaces are cool, in a fixed and unobtrusive spot, and easily accessible. To create your own wine storage area, stack up hexagonal terracotta drainage pipes to fit within the fireplace opening, being sure to have your lowest layer of pipes spread completely across the base of the hearth – this will prevent the pipes from 'spreading' once they become heavier with wine bottles.

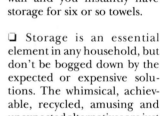

decorative storage. Paint tin trunks, restain old leather luggage or refurbish a truly authentic hat-box.

❏ Boxes of all sorts and sizes can become amusing and talked-about storage containers (or articles). Old wooden ammunition boxes, biscuit tins, sturdy paper cartons and slatted pine fruit boxes can be painted or decoupaged, and even shoe boxes made from very firm cardboard can be covered with fabric to become a practical and attractive storage container.

❏ Picture frames can be used as notice-board surrounds.

❏ Small wooden safety ladders, providing they have a flat top, can become ideal bedside tables. Single-sided old ladders

QUICK-FIX PROJECT
Brass luggage rack
A brass railway carriage luggage rack attached to the bathroom wall is an unexpected storage fitting. Replacing books with attractively folded towels is an option if long visits to the bathroom need to be discouraged!

with frame and rungs of dowel can become discussion pieces when used as towel racks in a kitchen – lean them against a wall and you instantly have storage for six or so towels.

❏ Storage is an essential element in any household, but don't be bogged down by the expected or expensive solutions. The whimsical, achievable, recycled, amusing and unexpected alternatives are just waiting to be discovered.

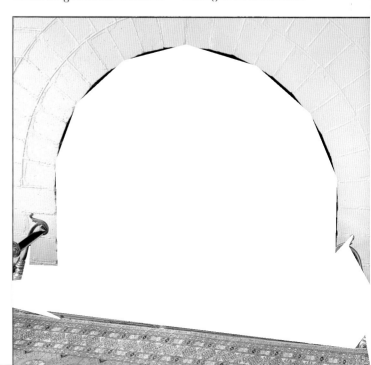

Finishing Touches

That great second-hand find isn't finished until you've added the decorative touches. If it's flair or dash you want, fittings like knobs and latches can really add that 'je ne sais quoi' to an otherwise quite ordinary piece.

A 'finishing touch' is quite literally that – whether you add bold red plastic knobs to a chest of drawers in a brightly coloured children's room, or install a very classy brass latch on a restored, natural-finish timber chest.

Decorative fittings are many-splendoured things and come in a vast range of different styles, colours and textures. Naturally, the style you choose will reflect the character of the piece itself, or even a room's general theme, personality or colour scheme. A modern piece often demands a modern treatment – for example, a smooth rounded style with no sharp edges, made from metal or plastic. This type of fitting is easy to clean and designed for safety.

A country-style piece often suits the more textured look of wood grain, which can be clear-stained or lightly oiled or waxed. You may decide to paint a wooden knob to match the overall finish of a piece, or even hand-paint or stencil on a design for that extra-special treatment.

If your piece is a genuine antique, you should enhance its distinctive style and character by selecting the appropriate fittings.

A selection of brass and chrome door knobs and latches

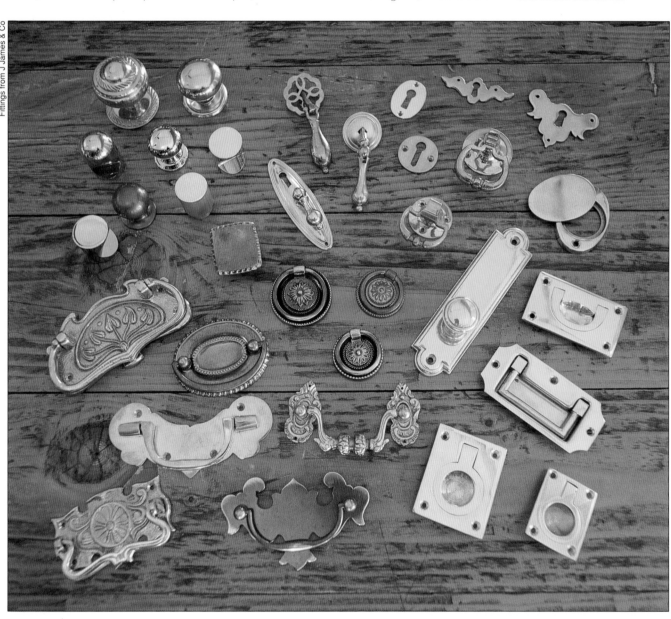

Fittings from J James & Co

SKILL CLASS
Nails and screws

NAILS

For accurate, well-finished work, nails alone do not normally make a strong enough joint. However, if the nails are angled in opposition to each other, a reasonable joint can be made. When used in conjunction with one of the modern woodworking adhesives, a very strong joint can be achieved.

When nailing two pieces of wood together, nail the smaller to the larger. Avoid nailing into hardwoods altogether: if you must, drill a pilot hole first, slightly smaller than the shank of the nail.

Removing nails

The claw hammer is used to remove partially driven nails. To avoid damaging the surface of the wood, place a small offcut under the hammer head before you start levering. Extract nails with a number of pulls rather than trying to do the job in one.

Use pincers to remove small nails and pins which are difficult to grip with the claw hammer, (e.g. nail without a head).

If a nail is impossible to remove, punch it below the surface of the wood and use filler to cover the hole, or carefully chip away some of the wood around the head until you can get a grip on the nail head with a pair of pincers.

Using a hammer

Take a firm grip at the end of the handle and form your arm into a right-angle, looking straight down on the work as you do so. Start the nail by tapping it lightly, keeping your wrist controlled but flexible and letting the hammer head do the work. Increase the power of your stroke slightly as the nail goes in but at no time let your arm waver – if you do, you will either miss or bend the nail. On well-finished work, remember not to drive nails right in – leave a bit protruding for the hammer and nail punch to finish off.

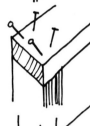

Use nails about 3 times as long as the workpiece. Always nail smaller to larger.

On rough work, clench nailed joints are much stronger.

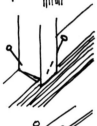

Skew-nailing is one of the best ways of securing a housing joint.

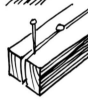

When nailing into end-grain, drive in nails at opposing angles.

Driving more than one nail along the same grain line risks splitting the wood.

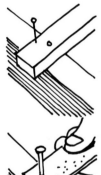

Nail small battens overlength to avoid splitting the ends. Saw or plane off the excess.

Small nails can be positioned with the aid of a cardboard holder.

Secret nailing. Prise up a sliver of timber with a chisel. Glue down after nailing.

SCREWS
Drilling screw holes

All screws must have pilot holes made before they can be driven home. For screws smaller than No. 6 gauge (3.5 mm) into softwood, make these with a bradawl. Drive it into the wood with its chisel point across the grain, to avoid splitting.

Screws larger than No. 6 gauge into hardwood and screws into softwood need two holes – one for the thread (the pilot hole) and one for the shank (the clearance hole). These must be made with a drill and bit.

When drilling pilot holes, mark the required depth on the drill bit with a piece of masking tape. This will tell you when to stop and cannot damage the workpiece should you overdrill.

As with nailing, where two pieces of wood are to be fixed together, screw the smaller to the larger. Drill the clearance hole right through the smaller piece so it is pulled down tight as the screw is driven home. If the clearance hole goes only part of the way through you will find it very hard to pull the top piece of wood down tight and may risk breaking or damaging the screw. Brute force should never be used – it indicates that either the thread hole or the shank hole is too small.

Driving screws

Always make sure that the tip of your screwdriver is in good condition and that it fits exactly into the slot in the screw head. A blade which is too narrow or rounded damages the slot, while too wide a blade damages the wood as the screw goes in.

As a time-saving alternative to the conventional screwdriver, a pump-action screwdriver works by converting downward movement of the sliding handle into rotation of the tip. So, simply by pushing hard, the screw is driven very quickly in or out of the wood (depending on the setting of the ratchet). Take extra care when using a pump-action screwdriver not to slip and injure yourself.

Countersinking

Countersinking is normally the easiest way of recessing screw heads flush with, or below the surface of the wood. The recess is made with a countersink bit after the clearance hole has been drilled, to the same depth as the countersunk screw head. Take particular care if you are countersinking with a power drill or the recess may accidentally become too large.

For some screw sizes, special bits are available to drill the thread hole, shank hole and countersink recess in one operation. Care should be taken, however, as they break easily.

Common types and uses

Countersunk screw: Used for general woodwork. The head sinks in flush with or slightly below the wood surface.

Crosshead screw: Used for general woodwork, but needs a special screwdriver which does not slip from the head.

Countersunk roundhead (raised head): Used for fixing door-handle plates and other decorative fittings with countersunk holes. The head is designed to be seen.

Roundhead screw: Used for fixing hardware fittings without countersunk holes.

Mirror (dome) screw: Used for fixing mirrors and bathroom fittings. The chromed cap threads into the screw head to hide the screw. Do not over-tighten.

Coach (or hexagon) head screw: Used for fixing heavy constructions together and heavy equipment to timbers. Tighten with a spanner.

Invisible (dowel) screw: Used for invisible joining of two pieces of timber.

Self-tapping (panel) screw: Used for fixing thin sheets of metal and plastic. Cuts its own thread as it is screwed in. Various types of head are available.

Particle (chip) board screw: Used for securing particle (chip) board and its derivatives.

Shelve it, stack it, stow it, store it! Shelving is one of the easiest and most versatile ways of dealing with domestic clutter. Place items on view or design a system to hide them away.

SHELVING IT

Good storage, as much as having good installations to handle it, is a state of mind and relates to a very human desire to put things away or hoard. Before choosing a suitable storage system for your lifestyle, there are a couple of points you should consider.

❑ Do you want to conceal things or display them? Most household items are well hidden away in cupboards and nooks, whereas some items, like collectables or ornaments, are possessions you would like to see.

❑ How often will you be using the stored items? Many seasonal items such as summer/winter clothes, blankets and eiderdowns, fans, portable heaters and Christmas decorations are likely to be used only at a certain time of the year.

Items used more frequently include tools, hobby equipment and clothes.

Things used daily must be stored in a handy place. These include cooking equipment, crockery, cutlery and glassware, daily clothes and shoes, toys, cleaning materials, study materials, videos, tapes, records and CDs, linen and so on. Books should be stored where they are easily accessible and away from any damp.

Most household items fit best in square and rectangular storage systems. Make sure you are happy and comfortable with the way your system works.

Shelving

The possibilities in shelving are enormous. Not only can you put objects on top of shelves but, with rails and hooks, the underside can also be utilised.

One of the most versatile installations is adjustable shelving for storage of just about anything. This type of shelving can cover a whole wall, or just a section of a wall. It can be fixed to timber-framed or brick walls.

Bookcases

Bookcases are a special form of shelving, and are always a point of interest in the home. Like shelving, bookcases come in various styles. To define where shelving stops and bookcases start is perhaps best done by examining what is on the shelves.

Alcoves

Look at wasted corners around the house. A popular storage idea for years has been to fit out the space between projections such as fireplaces and piers. The possibilities are endless. One such solution is to convert an alcove into two-tier hanging space in a bedroom, thus relieving the pressure on your everyday wardrobe. See Project 3 (Framing up an alcove) on page 34.

In other rooms alcoves can house shelving for books or treasures; they can include built-in loudspeakers which otherwise take up floor or shelf space; they can

Above: Bookshelves in the television/reading room with a pull-out swivel television, a shelf underneath for the VCR and cupboard doors that open out with pull-out trays for storage of video tapes. Glass cupboard doors protect a collection of old, rare books
Right: Hi-tech combination of desk and shelves with rubber caps that 'grab' the wall

Shelving is the staple of the storage system – it comes in all shapes, sizes and styles.

FREEDOM

APL

Graheme McIntosh Interiors

Clockwise from bottom left: Compact study/work area features a desk with pull-out leaf and a cupboard above for storage of stationery and books; Adjustable shelves in a kitchen cupboard with alcove shelves for display; Shelf unit used as a room divider; Shelf built in over a doorway for convenient storage of a television and VCR; Decorative wooden wall shelves for toiletries

Assess what you want in terms of materials for shelves and consider how you will attach them to the wall.

TIPSTRIP

SIMPLE BOOKSHELVES
To make this simple book storage system, place bricks or blocks no more than 750 mm apart, place timber over these and build them up to whatever height is required. The blocks can be concrete, clay bricks, cork blocks or anything else that may be stable. Shelves are best if they are at least 25 mm dressed (planed) timber. High shelves built like this should have the upper shelves anchored to the wall. An alternative is to slope each shelf and brick slightly backwards.

Laura Ashley

incorporate a small bar refrigerator, or a wine rack, or wood storage for the fireplace, or they can be converted into a linen cupboard.

Alcoves are common in many rooms, especially in older homes. They can be considered as the inside space of a cabinet or cupboard, ready to be fitted out in whatever manner is appropriate for your storage needs. It is a simple matter to mount a series of shelves in the space, in any of the methods described elsewhere in this book. This makes ideal storage for ornaments, books, games, pottery – even an open bar. It is also possible to include glass shelving for display purposes. The alcove may also have glass doors on its front face for protection against dust.

An alcove can simply have a door or doors fitted to the front to allow upright storage of vacuum cleaners, brooms, hanging clothes, or the like. Some converted alcoves have sophisticated architectural storage features, incorporating room themes such as arches, window

designs, corbelling or other features.

The trick with fitting out any alcove or similar area is to avoid building a second hefty frame which will eat up potential storage space. Thin jambs on either side, or sleek thin brackets should be sufficient.

It is important that the weight on the shelves can be adequately supported by the support or bracketing provided. The walls should be sound enough to take screws into timber studs, or to be plugged for fixing to masonry or plastered walls. Another problem, especially in older homes, is that of working around ornate skirtings and cornices. There may even be picture rails, dado panels, rails and vents that have to be taken into account. However, with care, you can work around all these features without destroying them (perhaps they could even be extended through the alcove fit-out as a continuation of the room's ornamentation).

Shelves for storage and display in the kitchen

Shelves in the living room for multipurpose storage

Wardrobes and built-ins

These days wardrobes are generally built-in, with sliding doors which include a full height mirror. These built-ins are an integral part of the house.

The fit-out of wardrobes has gone beyond a few drawers, some hanging space and shelves. Now wardrobe companies will supply a whole system that includes ample drawers, shelves and hanging space, often on several levels. Manufacturers also include wire basket storage systems which may be wheeled or fixed and are usually stackable; shoe storage; pull-out extra towel rails; tie and belt racks. Normally, the wardrobe will be internally lit, with an automatic switch, and may also include a dressing table-cum-mirror arrangement. The whole unit may even be built across the entrance to an otherwise poky en-suite or dressing room. Many are built of predrilled vertical members,

allowing the fittings to be changed to an infinite number of combinations as needs change, or as you accumulate more possessions.

Cabinets and cupboards

The ultimate in the furniture maker's art is that of attractive display cabinets. Often cabinets do not make best use of the space they occupy, but then that is not their primary function.

Cabinets would be amongst the most expensive forms of storage in that often solid wood is used, great detail in workmanship is displayed, and areas of glass, also expensive, abound. The level of finish is usually much better than that of the average built-in, with the fit of doors and attention to detail superior.

Cabinets are most often chosen to store and display collections of china, porcelain, art objects, crystal, and just about anything else of value. Because of the display aspect of cabinets, the contents are normally not crammed in as in other storage units.

IKEA

SKILL CLASS
Easy ways to go up the wall

Material	Finished thickness (mm)	Maximum span (mm)
solid dressed (planed) timber	19	900
solid dressed (planed) timber	31	1350
structural plywood	17	900
particle (chip) board	18	700
melamine-faced particle (chip) board	16	600
sheet glass		

A number of materials can be used for shelving. Our table on types of shelving provides a list of those in common use, with a suggested maximum span or bracket spacing for average loading.

SHELF (STAYED) BRACKETS

For supporting heavy loads, sometimes called gallows brackets. Welded steel brackets for shelving up to 300 mm wide can be purchased ready-made, or they can be constructed from timber to suit shelving up to any reasonable width (say 600 mm).

❑ To fix brackets to the wall, select a suitable spacing so as not to exceed the maximum span for the type of shelving to be used (see table).

❑ Strike a level line at the required height of the shelf.

❑ For timber-framed structures, brackets must be fastened to a solid stud using 12- or 14-gauge screws; on brick or masonry walls, drill and plug the wall for a screw fixing or alternatively a suitable masonry bolt will provide even more secure fixing for very heavy loads.

SHELF SUPPORTS

These are a simple method of providing support for adjustable shelving within a cabinet or wall unit. A series of holes to fit the pin of the shelf support, usually 5 mm to 6.5 mm in diameter, are drilled into the side members. Supports of metal, or coloured or clear

plastic come in a variety of patterns. It is essential that all of the holes are drilled at the same height within the unit. On a piece of firm timber, approximately 40 mm x 10 mm, mark out and drill the holes at the required spacing. Clamp this jig to the side members where holes are required, keeping the bottom to a fixed line marked on each member. Drill the holes to the depth required, using a depth-stop on the drill bit.

SHELF BRACKETS

For average loads. Available in galvanised steel or pressed metal in a variety of sizes to suit shelving up to 300 mm wide of solid timber, plywood or particle (chip) board. Again, strike a level line to indicate the height of the shelf and fix the brackets to this line with 10- or 12-gauge screws.

TIMBER BATTENS/ CLEATS

Where the end of a shelf butts up to a side wall, a timber batten/cleat can provide adequate support.

❑ Cut the batten/cleat from approximately 50 mm x 25 mm DAR (PAR) timber and mark a level line at the height of the shelf.

❑ Drill and plug the wall and secure the batten/cleat with 10- or 12-gauge screws.

METAL STANDARDS AND BRACKETS

Slotted metal uprights and adjustable brackets provide

adjustable shelving for average loads. Shelving is usually of 16 mm melamine-faced particle (chip) board or MDF in a variety of colours and widths from 150 mm to 300 mm. The shelves can also be of glass.

❑ To set up the system, select a suitable spacing for the uprights and locate secure fixing points on the wall. Strike a vertical line at each position and mark lightly. Mark the height to the bottom of the first upright and from this point level across and mark a point for the next and any subsequent ones. Using suitable screws, often provided with the system, fix the uprights to the wall at the positions marked.

❑ The brackets can now be fixed in the desired positions by means of two lugs which engage into the slots in the uprights.

LADDER BRACKET

The ladder bracket is a convenient way of giving support to multiple shelving where fixing points for other types of brackets or battens/cleats are not available. The brackets can be made to any depth up to 450 mm for the storage of linen and so on, or 600 mm if part of the space is to be used for the hanging of clothes. Brackets

can be made from 50 mm x 25 mm DAR (PAR) timber, and consist of uprights and intermediate rails spaced as required for the shelving. They are preferably dowelled together, and need only be nailed to the side walls as a complete unit at, say, four or five fixing points wherever they can be found.

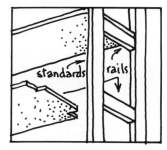

LADDER BRACKET
(for multiple shelving)

SLOTTED STANDARD
(with adjustable brackets)

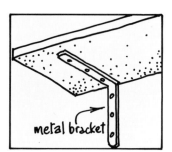

METAL BRACKET
(galvanised steel or pressed metal types)

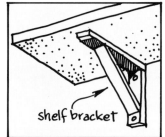

SHELF BRACKET
(for heavy loading timber or metal types)

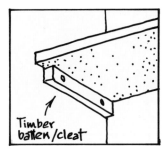

TIMBER BATTEN/CLEAT
(metal standards and brackets)

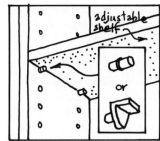

SHELF SUPPORT
(for adjustable shelving within units)

Framing up an alcove

Alcoves offer the perfect opportunity to make the most of otherwise small and cramped spaces.

This particular project is in a bedroom, where a solitary alcove originally made the room appear strangely offset. The space was used as additional hanging space for good clothes on two levels, as well as shoe and dress jewellery storage. The top hanging level is for seasonal or infrequently used clothes, and the lower provides ready access for more popular items. The idea was also to use two standard off-the-shelf doors to enclose the area.

STEP BY STEP

1 Firstly, measure up the space accurately so that you can draw a plan of the project. In this case, the alcove is 1380 mm wide, by a total of 2985 mm high. The total available depth is 440 mm. The alcove has an ornate cornice and an older style but plain 170 mm-high timber skirting. The floor is carpeted.

MATERIALS		
ITEM	DIMENSIONS (mm)	QUANTITY
softwood (pine or similar)	75 x 25	2 lengths (3.0 m), 4 lengths (1.5 m)
softwood (pine or similar)	50 x 25	1 length (1.5 m)
particle (chip) board	1500 x 240 x 19 thick 1500 x 650 x 15 thick	1 length 1 length
hollow core doors	size to fit	2
plastic-covered steel rod or similar	16 diameter	4 (400 mm)
saddle clips		8
butt hinges	75	3 per door
knobs		2
roller catches		2
aluminium strips	1.5 x 25 (600)	3 lengths
rubber doorstops		6
nails, screws and wall fixings as necessary		
undercoat and oil-based paint to finish		

SPECIAL TOOLS
hammer drill
jigsaw

TIME
Two weekends

2 The fitting-out involves fixing two doors to jambs, and the installation of two rail supports to carry the two levels of clothing rails at 1740 mm and 2790 mm from the floor.

Cut the two side frames (jambs) to size (in this case, standard 75 mm x 25 mm stock without a rebate was used). The thickness of the jamb is the same as the bottom skirting, so will sit on top. The jambs must be notched to a depth of 25 mm between 1500 mm and 1570 mm, and between 2550 mm and 2620 mm from the base to house the front rail supports. When the jambs are completed, they can be screwed to plugged walls or, if timber studs, to the timber frame.

3 To plug the wall, drill holes about 10 mm diameter with a tungsten carbide-tipped masonry bit in a hammer drill set on slow speed and hammer action. They should be in the middle of the jambs so that the plug is covered by the jamb. Smaller plugs can be used for finer work. Drive a soft piece of timber into each hole – then the nails or screws can be driven

in. This is a traditional method of plugging. Heavy-duty wall plugs or frame fixings (screws with integral plugs) can also be used and don't require such a large drill.

4 When secure, cut the two front rails of 75 mm x 25 mm timber to length and nail to the housings in the jambs. After marking with a spirit level, nail a similar pair at the same height to the rear wall, once again plugging the wall if necessary. This provides the basic structure for the storage space.

5 Cut 16 mm plastic-covered steel rods to length 1400 mm to fit between the front face of the rail support and the rear wall (hold in place using simple saddle clips). Purpose-made brass or other rail holders can also be used if preferred. Both rails are spaced with their centres at 295 mm from the side walls.

6 Lay a 1380 mm x 240 mm piece of 19 mm particle (chip) board across the skirtings to act as a shoe shelf. This should be painted with an undercoat and

finished with two coats of oil-based paint.

7 The doors now need to be fitted, one at a time. Butt hinges give the required clearance when the leaves are parallel and the door closed and therefore need to be let into the door and jamb. To fit the butt hinges to the doors, mark the position of the hinges on each door edge, one 150 mm from the top, one 200 mm from the bottom and one in the middle. Use a sharp chisel to remove a small amount of timber – just enough to allow the hinge flap to sit neat and flush in the door edge – then insert two screws for each hinge. It is best to predrill slightly with a smaller diameter drill bit before driving in the screws.

8 Support each door on small wedges to give the correct clearance over the carpeted floor, and mark in the position of the hinges on the jamb. Chisel out enough of the jamb to allow the hinge flap to fit flush as well, then hold the door in place and mark and drill the screw holes to get the screws started. Hang the door by inserting a screw, top and bottom. Before putting in all screws, make sure that the door closes properly and is correctly aligned. If not, make adjustments until it is right, using an adjacent screw hole.

Repeat this procedure for the other door. When both doors have been fitted, check that they have sufficient clearance, and that the meeting of the two door edges is parallel and neat. The meeting stiles may need to be slightly bevelled to the rear if the fit is close, to allow the doors to shut. When all is well, insert the remaining screws in both doors. Fit the decorative knobs of your choice to the doors.

Fit two catches and keepers to the central rail support and to each door and block them out so that the doors will fit flush across their face.

9 The doors are only 2350 mm high, thus leaving a gap above of about 630 mm, which is filled using a sheet of 15 mm particle (chip) board. But first fix a small batten/cleat of 50 mm x 25 mm timber to the door jambs above each door by screwing in place, 15 mm in from the front.

The particle (chip) board must be cut to suit the cornice profile. A handy tool for this job is a profile gauge. Otherwise, make a cardboard template to suit the cornice and then transpose this onto the two top corners of the particle (chip) board as a cutting guide.

10 When ready, nail or screw the particle (chip) board to the battens/cleats and finish flush with the jamb. Punch and fill any nail holes, then seal and undercoat using oil-based paints to stop the grain rising. Finish the doors similarly with an oil-based undercoat and top coats.

11 All remaining surfaces should be prepared for painting by lightly sanding and dusting down before the interior is painted out. For a finishing touch, a wallpaper strip was added around the room just under the cornice, thus marrying the infilled alcove to the rest of the room.

12 For storage of earrings, screw three 600 mm-long rails of 25 mm x 1.5 mm aluminium to the inside face of one of the doors, using rubber doorstops as spacers.

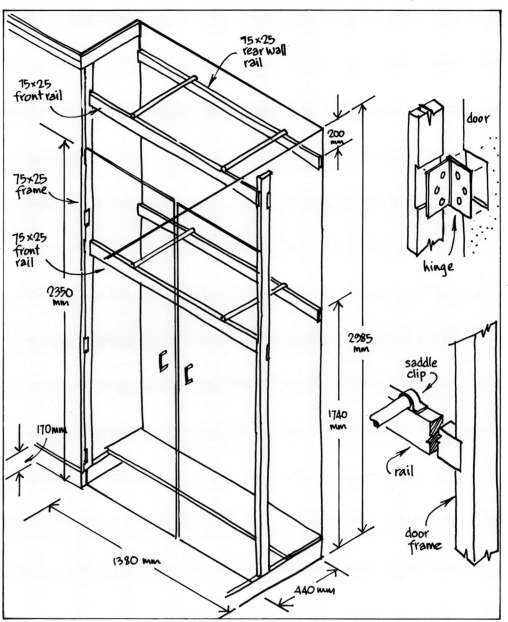

75 x 25 rear wall rail

75 x 25 front rail

75 x 25 frame

75 x 25 front rail

2350 mm

170 mm

1380 mm

440 mm

200 mm

2985 mm

1740 mm

door

hinge

saddle clip

rail

door frame

The living room is usually the room most on show to visitors – it is, in many ways, your indoor home entertainment area. Make your storage system visually appealing, easily accessible and compatible with your lifestyle.

LIVING SPACES

Your furniture and especially your storage units should be as visually appealing as possible, yet still comfortable and user-friendly.

To establish your storage needs, consider who will be using the room and what its main function will be. Do you want permanently fixed storage or do you want to rearrange the room from time to time? Is there a natural focus in the room? Could a collection of objects or a large piece of furniture – such as a bookcase, cabinet or wall unit – be incorporated to display a prized collection? Is the living area mainly a family room?

Also consider how well any new storage ideas will fit into your living room. Ask yourself:

❑ Is it the right size?
❑ Does it harmonise with other elements in the room? Functional furniture, such as the television and stereo system, is best kept behind closed doors in a unit or cabinet, or at least in a part of the room where they will be relatively safe from the children's occasional rough and tumble. Treasured items, on the other hand, should be on display. Your antiques, for example, could be a focal point in a glass-fronted cabinet or Georgian chest-on-chest. Books are classic adornments and may range from your toddler's picture books to large-format coffee table books.

The three basic types of storage to choose from are freestanding, movable furniture (sideboards, chest, cabinets, bookcases and industrial shelving); built-in shelves and cupboards; and modular units. Modular units are specifically designed to fit flush against the wall or to form a solid dividing unit. Keep the finish simple and continue any moulding of baseboards across the top and bottom of new fittings to maintain a regular appearance in the room. A wall unit is certainly a neat solution for both storage and display. In large rooms, a modular unit could be freestanding; in a townhouse, built-in shelving and cupboards can exploit otherwise wasted space.

The most practical style of shelving unit has cupboards below and a deep shelf at waist height. The cupboards could be deep enough to hold a filing cabinet if the room doubles as a study, and a television set could be fitted on a tray for easy viewing.

Adjustable shelving is an added benefit if you have lots of books and collectables. Avoid placing bookshelves near fireplaces or in direct sunlight. Valuable books should be protected behind glass.

Glass shelving is ideal for contemporary homes or where light is at a premium.

Records, cassettes and CDs need support at regular intervals. For convenience, short but deep stackable cubes are perfect.

Clockwise from bottom left (page 36):
Shelves built into a staircase wall; Built-in cupboards with glass doors for display and storage of ornaments, glass and silverware; Portable wine storage next to an ornamental fireplace

Clockwise from right: Hi-tech portable entertainment centre; Wooden storage unit; Freestanding unit for multipurpose storage; Adjustable bookshelves

Modularack

FREEDOM

TIPSTRIP

FUN SOLUTIONS
As an alternative to the standards, try improvising storage ideas – it may save money and will give your living room a sense of personality. Lateral thinking pays dividends here.
❏ A drinks trolley by the side of a sofa to hold glasses, trays, ice bucket and so on.
❏ Industrial steel trolleys for storing stereo, television and video equipment.
❏ Baskets, chests and wicker trunks for storing books, magazines, or children's toys.
❏ Surround a sofa with drawers, shelves and cupboards – the tops of which could double as side tables.
❏ Hinge two ladders together and place lengths of wood across each corresponding rung to create an A-frame shelving system.

Living room, lounge, parlour, salon, drawing room, front room – the variety of names given to living rooms reflects a variety of uses. Generally, they can be divided into two distinct types of room: a formal setting for use only when entertaining, and the more relaxed centre for family life.

FREEDOM

FREEDOM

FREEDOM

Project 4

Entertainment centre

This modular stereo and home entertainment centre can easily be expanded or adapted to suit your needs. It has been cleverly designed to accommodate equipment as well as an extensive collection of CDs, records, videos and cassettes.

The project consists of three units which have a total width of just over 1500 mm. Although the centre is modular, it is also relatively low level, and a single top and kickboard draws all three units together.

The centre is built on a slight plinth, and involves a minimum of carpentry complications. Commercial connection fittings have been used – these are strong and save the otherwise extensive dowelling and gluing procedures; they have the added benefit of being easy to dismantle. The main cabinet is built of veneered particle (chip) board, edge-veneered on the front, with solid cabinet timber drawer fronts, kickboard and top edging.

Note: Cabinet timber refers to any fine-quality, dressed (planed) furniture-grade timber of your choice.

STEP BY STEP

Buy all the materials, and have them ready for use. Treat the veneered board with care to avoid damage. If possible, make the total number of units you require at once. This will make the process much faster as you can set up a mini production line.

1 Mark out the sides of the cabinet on the particle (chip) board sheets. The depth of all sides, bottoms, shelves and the top is 400 mm, so cut the particle (chip) board into 400 mm-wide strips for convenience. The sides are 825 mm high. Cut the particle (chip) board sheets with a circular saw for the best results. When cutting with a circular saw, put the best side face down, as the saw 'cuts up' and gives a very clean edge on the underside. To guide the saw, clamp a straightedge on the panel to be cut, allowing for the distance between the saw base edge and the blade. Use scraps of softwood to protect the board when clamping. Once all the sheets have been cut, cut a small 40 mm deep x 70 mm notch out of the bottom front of each panel to later accommodate the kickboard.

2 Before proceeding any further, mark on the inside cabinet the position of the shelves and the tops of the shelf supports. The basic positions of the spacing used in this project are (from the top):

19 mm – underside of top frame
170 mm – top of top shelf
189 mm – underside of top shelf, shelf support
350 mm – top of middle shelf
369 mm – underside of middle shelf, shelf support
731 mm – top of bottom shelf
750 mm – underside of bottom shelf
825 mm – base of side

The tops of the drawer guides can also be marked where applicable. For example, in the unit with just one middle drawer, mark the top of the guide at 120 mm above the

MATERIALS

Quantities are for building three units. This can be varied for more or less units. This project was made using 19 mm particle (chip) board but 16 mm thick board can also be used with the necessary adjustments to dimensions.

ITEM	DIMENSIONS (mm)	QUANTITY
hardwood-veneered particle (chip) board – cabinet	1220 x 2440 x 19	2 sheets
plywood – backs and drawer bottoms	1220 x 2440 x 3	1 sheet
cabinet timber DAR (PAR) – drawer fronts for large drawers	200 x 25	1 length (1 m)
cabinet timber DAR (PAR) – front top member of cabinet, kickboard and drawer fronts for small drawers	100 x 25	2 lengths (1.5 m) 1 length (2.1 m)
cabinet timber DAR (PAR) – rear top of cabinet	75 x 25	1 length (1.5 m)
cabinet timber DAR (PAR) – edging of the top	25 x 25	1 length (1.8 m) 2 lengths (0.6 m)
cabinet timber DAR (PAR) – large drawer sides and backs	150 x 19	1 length (2.7 m)
cabinet timber DAR (PAR) – small drawer sides and backs	75 x 19	1 length (2.4 m)
cabinet timber DAR (PAR) – drawer guides	12 x 25	2 lengths (2.4 m)
cabinet timber glazing bead – optional	12 x 19	2 lengths (3.6 m)
cabinet timber DAR (PAR) – shelf battens/cleats	12 x 12	1 length (2.4 m)
iron-on veneer to suit		8 m
connection fittings		24 in total (8 per unit)
double-headed connecting screws		8
handles to suit		6
record dividers (optional)		
stain and polyurethane finish as required		

SPECIAL TOOLS

This project could be built using hand tools, but power tools will save you a lot of time.
circular saw (with a fine-cutting tungsten-carbide tip blade)
router
jigsaw
power drill
sash cramps (optional)

TIME

Three or four weekends, depending on finish

Ironing on veneer

Drawer ready to be assembled

Fixing top drawer on guides

shelf immediately below it. This gives a 1 mm clearance between the drawer bottom and the shelf.

3 Cut to length the shelf supports and drawer guides and fix in place. The shelf supports in this case were simply 12 mm x 12 mm cabinet timber strips cut to 350 mm (that is, 50 mm short of the front) and at 45°, and glued and nailed in place. An alternative would be to drill holes and use plastic or metal shelf supports instead. If the shelves were to be housed in the sides, the housings should be routed or cut out to a depth of 5 mm at this stage.

4 The drawer guides are 19 mm x 12 mm cabinet timber cut to 385 mm, and must be accurately glued and nailed (or screwed) to the sides. (You may prefer to fit the drawer guides when the drawers are ready, to double-check that the position is right.)

5 Mark and cut out the bottom shelf, 400 mm deep by 462 mm wide. When finished this will give a total width of 500 mm for the whole unit.

6 Mark and cut rear and front top members of cabinet from

75 mm x 25 mm and 100 mm x 25 mm cabinet timber. These are also 462 mm long.

7 The bottom shelf and the two top framing members can be fixed to each side using connection fittings. These consist of male and female blocks which are screwed to the underside of the horizontal members and the corresponding position on the sides. When brought together, the coarse joining screw draws the two pieces tightly together. In all, eight connectors are needed for each cabinet.

Once in place, the position on the sides is easily marked by aligning the horizontal members with the sides. When these are set up, they can be assembled and dismantled if necessary.

8 Cut the backs to size – slightly less than the width and height of the cabinet to ensure that they are not seen. It is important to have good access to the rear of the stereo components for connecting, and good air circulation for cooling. For this reason, large neat holes are cut in the rear ply. They roughly follow the opening size, but the corners are rounded. Lightly nail the

backs to the rear of each cabinet, carefully aligning the cabinet to ensure that all corners are completely square. This may be temporary only to allow for dismantling and staining (see step 15). The plywood will act as a brace and stiffen up the cabinet. The bottom shelf can now also be drilled for the record dividers.

9 Screw a piece of 100 mm x 25 mm cabinet timber to the rear top framing member of one of the cabinets. This accommodates a four- or six-outlet electrical power board into which all the appliances can be plugged (so that only one electrical lead runs down to the power point).

10 The front edges of the particle (chip) board cabinets can now be covered in iron-on veneer to hide the end grain. The veneer strips are normally about 2-3 mm wider than necessary; cut them to length first. Heat up the edge of the particle (chip) board by running a hot iron along it over a piece of brown paper. Then place veneer on the edge and repeat the procedure. Follow along with a soft piece of timber to ensure good adhesion to the particle (chip) board. Any spots

that fail to adhere can be reheated and stuck again. Trim off excess veneer with a utility knife and sand the edges smooth.

Now cut the intermediate shelves 462 mm wide out of the 400 mm particle (chip) board panels. The front edge of these also needs to be edge-veneered to match the rest of the cabinet. The whole cabinet is now ready for sanding and finishing, which happens in a few steps time.

11 The next job is to make the drawers. These are perhaps the most difficult part of the project, even though they are not dovetailed and otherwise avoid tricky joinery. Power tools were used to minimise the time and work involved. Prefabricated drawers can also be used, with some adjustment made to the size of the whole unit for the correct fitting.

There are two drawer sizes, the larger size for compact discs and video tapes, and the smaller size for audio cassettes.

❏ Large-sized drawers: The fronts of the two larger drawers are made of 200 mm x 25 mm cabinet timber cut down to 158 mm exactly. This will give about a 1 mm clearance top and bottom between the shelves. The sides and back are made of 150 mm x 19 mm cabinet timber, which finishes at 141 mm x 12 mm. The back is cut down to 130 mm.

Groove the drawer front and sides between 7 mm and 10 mm to accept the 3 mm plywood drawer bottom. This is easiest to do with a power saw with a tungsten-tipped blade set to a shallow depth (about 5 mm). Also groove the sides between 99 mm and 119 mm on the outside to accept the drawer guides already fixed to the cabinet. This channel is easiest to cut with a router and a 12 mm straight bit (set to cut 8 mm deep).

Rebate the drawer front on the back edges to accept the sides. The depth is 12 mm, the same as the thickness of the sides, and is designed to enable the side to be nailed into the end grain of the front, rather than nailing through the front. This groove should only go high enough to accommodate the side, thus leaving the top continuous.

Assemble each drawer with 25 mm panel pins and adhesive. Fit the back of the drawer above the bottom groove to allow the plywood bottom to be slid in place once the drawer has been constructed. Cut the drawer bottom to suit, slide it in position and nail the back of the bottom to the back of the drawer using small flat-head (roundhead) nails.

If not done previously, fit the drawer guides into the cabinet, and try each drawer to ensure it runs smoothly. If necessary, adjust the guides to suit.

❏ Small-sized drawers: The cassette drawers are constructed in a similar way using the smaller sized timbers.

12 The insides of the drawers can be fitted with dividers if desired. The cassette drawer will hold three cassettes across with a little extra space for head cleaning or other equipment. The CD drawer also holds three CDs across.

13 The table top to cover all three units is made of the same veneered particle (chip) board, but in this case is edged with 25 mm x 25 mm dressed (planed) timber of the same species. Apply the edging to the front edge and sides, and mitre it to the corners. This involves accurately cutting a 45° angle at the two front corners so that when assembled, the timber will show no end grain. Glue and nail the edging to the edge of the particle (chip) board, and punch and fill the nails. Use sash cramps to help hold the edge in place if necessary. For a more decorative effect, the edge can be routed to any number of edge treatments to match existing furniture, or to

simply round off the exposed edge. In this case, a rounding-over bit was used.

14 Fashion the front kickboard out of 100 mm x 25 mm cabinet timber, cut down to 70 mm, and screw-fix along the top of the kickboard with brown snap-on screw covers to hide the screw heads.

15 At this stage all the components are ready for finishing. To do this, it is best to totally dismantle the units, identifying each piece so that you know which unit it came from. Take each piece individually and carefully sand the edges and face using #120 paper. Remove all splinters, irregularities and pencil marks, being careful not to sand through the veneer. If staining, carefully apply the stain to all visible faces, wiping off any excess (follow the instructions on the tin).

16 Reassemble each unit, permanently nailing on backs and keeping the top, drawers and kickboard separate. Apply the recommended number of

finishing coats – in this case, a furniture-grade polyurethane was used.

17 When dry, the units can be joined using double-headed screw connectors – this will ensure they stay together and in alignment. Hold the cabinets together with a clamp while drilling for connectors, using scraps of softwood to protect the finish. The top can then be fixed to the units by screwing from the underside of the top framing members into the table top. Drill the holes in the cabinets slightly oversize, so that they will accommodate any slight movement in the top. Fix the kickboard to the rebate.

18 Fit the drawer-pulls or handles to the drawers. If the handles you are using are fixed from the inside, fit a little block under the fixing screws in the drawer bottom to ensure that cassettes or CDs do not get damaged by being in contact with the fixings. As an alternative, recess fixings into the drawer fronts by counter-boring.

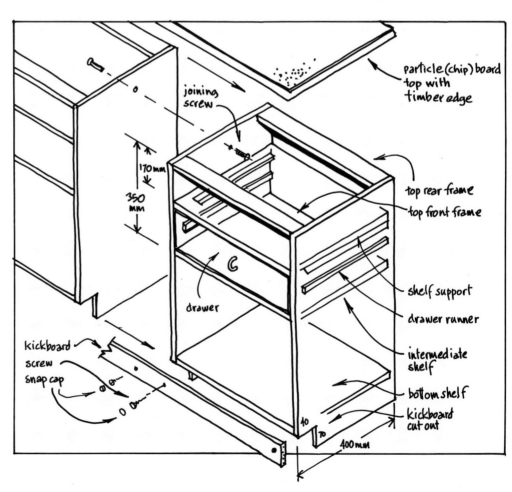

Flexibility is the key to successful storage in double-duty rooms and multipurpose areas. This need not result in makeshift mayhem. These stylish space-savers have been designed to make the most of in-between areas.

MULTIPURPOSE AREAS

There are so many ways to keep things in order and easily accessible – be inventive and resourceful with every little space you have.

Entrances

One area which needs to be flexible is the hallway, and as this is where visitors gain their first impressions, it is logical to give thought to its design and fittings. If possible, there should be at least one chair and a table large enough to take parcels, letters, magazines, a telephone, message pads and directories. A long, stepped bookcase can combine all three functions of table, seating and storage. Install handy hooks on the wall for coats and scarves, and a stand for umbrellas (a revamped Victorian hallstand can make an interesting talking-point).

In long or large corridors, there are obvious places for fitting in extra storage: for example, walls can be lined with units to take any excess household paraphernalia. China and glassware should be safely stored on the top shelf.

Wall-mounted fittings will occupy less space than freestanding pieces of furniture, and you may be able to use irregularities in the shape of the room to create an alcove with shelving for books, or, with the addition of sliding doors and some hooks or rails, a small cupboard for outdoor gear.

Thought should also be given to entrances at the back of the house. In many houses this is the service entry and, as such, there needs to be provision for the storage of prams, baskets, sporting equipment, outdoor toys, wet-weather gear or maybe even gardening implements.

Again, heavy-duty hooks hammered or screwed into solid walls could carry many of these items. One idea is to hang fishing rods, complete with reels, horizontally above doors – this way they become a decorative addition as well.

Study/guest room

Another room which often does double duty is the study/guest room. Storage can be organised to take up little space to enable the inclusion of a sofa bed or divan and a decent-sized desk. Whether you are using a whole room, or part of one, try to fit in the maximum amount of storage. An easily accessible filing system to keep papers and correspondence in some logical order should be a priority. Remember that items which are frequently used should be kept within easy reach.

Open shelving can be installed on the walls above or behind the desk. Deep drawers in desks, cupboards or wall units can be used for suspension files. A common practice is to use a laminate-finished desk surface to span a pair of two-drawer filing cabinets. This combines work space and storage in one.

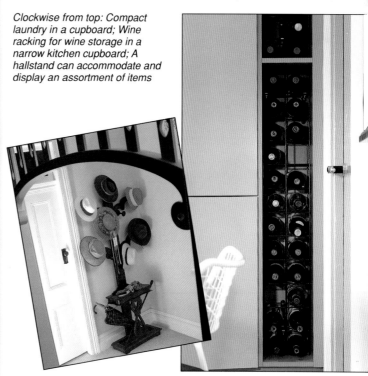

Clockwise from top: Compact laundry in a cupboard; Wine racking for wine storage in a narrow kitchen cupboard; A hallstand can accommodate and display an assortment of items

Linen cupboard for storage of bath towels, blankets and assorted linen

Full-length sliding doors or screens will allow you to close off the work area and to use the room for other purposes.

Books are an important part of any study and have certain storage requirements. They can deteriorate in areas of high humidity, gather dust and will turn yellow if exposed to direct sunlight. Books can be quite heavy, so ensure shelving is strong enough to hold their weight. Adjustable shelving will accommodate almost any type of tome, be it a directory, journal, coffee table book or large folder.

Bookshelves can be custom-built and cover a wall or walls to frame a sofa or stretch up and around doors and windows, giving a sense of perspective to the room. When guests come to stay it is easy to hide the working spaces and shelves of textbooks with a series of pull-up blinds (see quick-fix project). These can be dropped down for the duration of the stay and then raised for work to begin again. If the room is not big enough for a full-sized bed, consider a sofa bed. For

simple convenience put a couple of brass hooks on the back of the door for hanging clothes or, even better, why not try your hand at making our fabric shelves (Project 5) on page 43.

It is not only the study where a desk may be needed: it can be useful to have a pull-out desk or a flap at the end of a workbench in the kitchen for writing lists, or resting a recipe book on.

QUICK-FIX PROJECT
Pull-up blinds
The principle of these blinds is an old and good one. The front of the shelves is covered with fabric cut and sewn to fit the dimensions of the shelves. At evenly spaced intervals up the inside, casings are stitched across the blind, through which thin timber battens/cleats are slotted. Metal eye hooks are screwed into these battens/ cleats through the fabric in straight rows up the back of the blind, about 35 cm in from the edge of the blind and in the centre. The top of the fabric is tacked onto a timber batten/ cleat, which is then screwed onto the outside top front of the shelves. Screw one more eyehook into the supporting bracket at the top of each row of hooks. Cords are fastened to the lowest hook in each row, then threaded through the eyehooks, taken to one side and fastened onto a cleat. The blind moves up and down by pulling or releasing the cords.

Stack 'N' Store. Props from Derek Scott, Sandy de Beyer

Clever cupboards

If you do not have enough floor space to designate to utility areas like the laundry, there are simple but effective ways to disguise utilitarian facilities in your living spaces. Any long cupboard space can be used for brooms, mops, vacuum cleaners and outdoor gear. With a laundry, all you need is space for a washing machine, dryer and a wash tub or sink. The area does not need to be large, indeed a laundry works most efficiently when the spaces between equipment is not great (see Project 10, Laundry in a cupboard on page 60). Other space-saving possibilities include hanging canvas laundry bags or fabric shelves, cupboard doors that fold down to become table surfaces, and a fold-away ironing board. For another clever cupboard idea, see our Sewing centre project (Project 6 on page 44).

Under the stairs, up in the attic

It can be useful to take a fresh look at spaces that have never been used before for

Understair storage

storage. Stairs are an example. The understairs area is popular for storage, especially in small terrace houses, as it is often already partly enclosed and is surprisingly large. This area is easily converted into storage for luggage, sports equipment, firewood, wine, linen, and so on. The trick is to make sure that items stored at the rear, which is often over a metre from the front, are still accessible. Here, a good idea is to build a

Fabric shelves

These fabric shelves are ideal for a dual-purpose room which is short on space.

STEP BY STEP

1 With right sides facing, stitch stripe print pieces together along short edges to form one long strip. Press seam open. Press under 1 cm at remaining short edges, top-stitch and edgestitch to finish.

2 Fold strip every 30 cm to form five double-thickness open-backed shelves, with four single-thickness backs in between. Press.

3 With right sides facing, pin one small check print square to top, back and lower edges of one shelf side. 1 cm seam allowance at front edge of square will extend past finished shelf front. Clipping into corners, stitch around top, back and lower edges to form shelf side. Press. Repeat for other seven squares to form entire shelf unit.

4 With right sides facing, pin one large check print piece to side of shelf unit around front, back and lower edges. Large check print piece will extend 31 cm above top of shelf unit to form top hanging section. Clipping into corners, stitch around front, back and lower edges to enclose all seam

allowances. Trim seams and turn to right side. Press. Repeat for other side.

5 With right sides facing, stitch top edges of large check print pieces together to form top hanging section. Press seam open.

6 With right sides facing, stitch small check print rectangle to top hanging section along front edge. Clipping into corners, stitch side edges of rectangle to side edges of top shelf, enclosing all seam allowances. Trim seams, turn to right side. Press.

7 Press under 1 cm along back edges of top hanging section to enclose remaining seam allowances. Slipstitch together to finish.

8 Insert five rectangles of hardboard into open backs of shelves to complete shelf unit. Top hanging section should then be suspended from an appropriate wall bracket.

series of wheeled trolleys that roll into the space, are covered by attractive false panelling and, when something is needed, can be wheeled out and are easily accessible.

Gaining access to the attic can be as simple as installing a ladder – a range of practical attic ladders is available commercially. They are simple to pull down and store in the attic space themselves.

Underfloor storage

While it cannot be recommended to completely fill the subfloor area of the house with storage, because of ventilation, there is nevertheless plenty of scope for some storage there. It may not even have to be accessible through the tiny side door either. Items stored underfloor could include wine with access via a hatch or trapdoor, or more popularly floor safes for valuables, covered by a rug or, better still, carpet tiles.

Open up your attic for extra storage

MATERIALS	
ITEM	**QUANTITY**
115 cm wide large check print cotton fabric	2 m
115 cm wide stripe print cotton fabric	2.20 m
115 cm wide small check print cotton fabric	1.50 m
rectangles of hardboard (39 cm x 29 cm)	5

PATTERN
Cut two rectangles of large check print 152 cm x 32 cm for outside panels and top. Cut two rectangles of stripe print 212 cm x 42 cm for shelves and back. Cut eight squares of small check print 32 cm x 32 cm for inside panels, and cut one rectangle of small check print 62 cm x 32 cm for inside top. 1 cm seams allowed.

Project 6

Sewing centre

𝑇𝑇𝑇

This neat fold-away sewing centre has ample storage for not only a sewing machine, but also an overlocker, shelves of patterns, sewing accessories and other odds and ends.

This clever cupboard idea is based on a simple upright cabinet that takes no more room than a bookcase, and folds away in one or two easy steps.

The overall cupboard is 1070 mm wide as built (to fit in a corner) by 2070 mm high, and is a total of only about 350 mm deep with the doors shut. When open it reveals seven shelves for storage, and a sewing table 1220 mm x 600 mm. Our project was made from 19 mm particle (chip) board, but the sizes can easily be adjusted to other commonly available board thicknesses. It is made by simple carpentry, with no complex joints involved, and is finished with plastic laminate sheet glued to the particle (chip) board.

STEP BY STEP

You will need a considerable amount of room to build the unit, as the components are fairly large. It will be built on its face and then turned over.

1 Start by building the plinth on which the unit stands. This is made of 19 mm particle (chip) board which will be laminated later, with other surfaces. The size of the base is 1058 mm wide by 285 mm deep by 160 mm high. Cut two pieces of particle (chip) board 1058 mm x 160 mm, and three at 247 mm x 160 mm. Glue and nail (or screw) the base together, with one of the shorter pieces nailed as a centre support or stiffener.

2 Measure and cut the two side panels. They are 311 mm wide by 1910 mm high. Put the two sides together, and mark on each the position of shelves. The sequence from the top of the cabinet to the top of each shelf is 245 mm, 425 mm, 615 mm, 920 mm, 1315 mm and 1685 mm. Square across each piece at this level.

3 Measure and cut the top and bottom, both 311 mm wide by 1020 mm long. Cut the back out of hardboard to the size 1910 mm x 1058 mm. This forms the basis of the carcase. Also measure and cut six shelves out of the 19 mm particle (chip) board, each 225 mm wide by 1020 mm long.

4 Assemble the main outside of the carcase (face down) by gluing and nailing (or screwing) the sides to the top and bottom. Use PVA adhesive and 50 mm thin bullet-head nails.

While the cabinet is in this position, glue and nail or screw the shelves where marked. On the outside of each panel, draw a line corresponding with the half thickness of the shelves to give you a nailing guide. From the top, these lines would be at 254 mm, 434 mm, 624 mm, 929 mm, 1324 mm and 1694 mm. When nailing the shelves in position, align them to the upturned back of the cabinet for a well-aligned joint.

5 When all the shelves are in position, nail the back onto the cabinet with small flat-head (roundhead) nails, ensuring that the cabinet is held square. The hardboard will act as sheet bracing.

6 It is necessary to install a 50 mm x 25 mm softwood support to the underside of the shelf to be laminated; the table will be hinged to this shelf at 1295 mm from the top. Glue and screw the support from the particle (chip) board into the side grain of the softwood, which itself is secured to the sides of the cabinet by screwing or nailing and gluing. This will stop the shelf from bending with the considerable weights that will be placed on it. Similarly, screw a 75 mm x 25 mm batten/cleat to the underside of the top of the cabinet, 16 mm in from the front. Once the softwood front

MATERIALS

ITEM	DIMENSIONS (mm)	QUANTITY
particle (chip) board:		
– sides, shelves and plinth	2400 x 1200 x 19 thick	2 sheets
– front doors (prefinished and cut to size)	2100 x 600 x 19 thick	2 sheets
– table top	1220 x 600 x 19 thick	1 sheet
hardboard	1200 x 2100 x 3 thick	1 sheet
softwood DAR (PAR):		
– table leg	150 x 25	1 length (0.9 m)
– top and rear batten/cleat	75 x 25	2 lengths (1.2 m)
– shelf support	50 x 25	1 length (1.2 m)
– cabinet edging	25 x 25	2 lengths (2.1 m)
		1 length (2.4 m)
polyurethane (gloss)		
laminate	2100 x 650	1 sheet
	1220 x 900	1 sheet
matching laminate edging		4.8 m
iron-on edge veneer		6 m
cam-type sash lock		1
small magnetic catches		4
piano hingeing (600 mm)		1 length
butt hinge (75 mm)		1
overlay hinges for 19 mm doors (3 left-hand/3 right-hand)		6
door knobs of your choice		2
self-adhesive rubber doorstops (10 mm)		2
adhesive, nails and screws to suit		

SPECIAL TOOLS
laminate knife (double-sided, tungsten-tipped scriber)
laminate trimmer (router with laminate trimming bits) or a selection of flat files (coarse to fine)

TIME
Three weekends

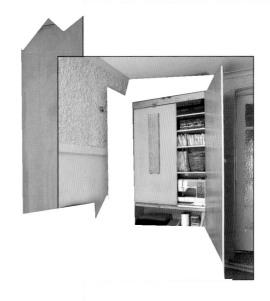

13 The shelf at 1295 mm from the top is also laminated on its top and front edge as it will undergo much harsh treatment (this shelf is the table extension onto which the sewing machine and any other bits and pieces are pushed). Cut the front edge strip to size (wide in height but in this case accurate in length), and glue it into place. Trim to a flat surface with the top of the shelf.

The laminate for the shelf has to be cut to fit exactly to the back edge and the two sides. The front edge can hang over by 2 mm to allow trimming to size when it is glued. Glue the laminate as before and when in place finish it off at 45° to 60° to the edge with a file or a laminate trimmer.

14 The final laminating job is that of the table top and edges. This needs to have all four edges laminated first, and then the top laminated to finish over the edges. It is also finished at 45° to give a safe smooth working surface and edge.

15 The dressed (planed) 25 mm x 25 mm front softwood edgings are actually dressed (planed) to 19 mm x 19 mm and can be glued and nailed (or screwed) to the front edge of the particle (chip) board to give an attractive finished appearance. As they will be butting against your new laminate on the outside faces, precoat them with polyurethane to avoid accidentally getting any coating on the new laminate.

16 To attach the table leg to the table, screw it to the underside of the table with the butt hinge. It is important that the flap of the hinge faces towards the cupboard so that when the table is raised, the leg will automatically fold against the bottom of the table. If correctly cut, the top of the table will be at 760 mm, which is normally a comfortable height to work at.

17 Fix the table top to the left side of the cupboard with a continuous piano hinge, screwed first to the table edge, and then to the shelf.

edges are installed, this will be 35 mm back from the front. This panel is designed to take the cam-type sash lock that will hold the table in a vertical position when the cabinet is closed up.

7 Also cut to length a 75 mm x 25 mm length of softwood to make the batten/cleat, which is fixed to the top back of the cabinet to act as an anchor that can be screwed to the wall. The two sides are trimmed off at 45°. Screw the batten/cleat to the cabinet from the underside of the top panel into the side grain of the timber.

8 The entire interior of the cabinet and the shelves can now be coated with polyurethane to give an easy-care, hard-wearing surface. Gloss was chosen as this also brings out the cork-like texture of the particle (chip) board. Give the whole at least two, preferably three, coats. Do not coat the front edge of the shelves or the top surface of the shelf that will be laminated (see below).

9 The next task is to cut out the table top to the size 1218 mm x 598 mm. The width can be increased or decreased if desired, but the height must

remain at 1218 mm to fit inside the cabinet, unless the shelf heights are also adjusted. Once the table top is cut out it is ready for laminating, which will bring the total size to 1220 mm x 600 mm.

10 The first surface to laminate will be the exposed side of the cupboard (you may find it easiest to have the cabinet laying on its opposite side for this).

Laminating with plastics should be done carefully as the materials are relatively expensive. Cut the laminate to about 2 mm oversize all the way round (this allows accurate trimming when the laminate is fully glued) using a laminate knife. This is run along a straight edge repeatedly (front and back) until a sufficiently deep groove is cut for the sheet to be easily snapped.

11 Cut a series of dowels or thin scrap timber strips to lay across the worktop to separate the laminate from the particle (chip) board while it is adjusted into place. Make sure both laminate and particle (chip) board are dust free, then evenly spread a thin layer of contact adhesive (using the supplied applicator) on the laminate and then on the particle (chip)

board. Being a contact adhesive, it works best when it is just dry. Test this with the back of your hand in one or two spots. The adhesive will also look dull rather than wet.

When tack free, lay the previously cut dowels on the side about 300 mm apart, and then position the plastic laminate on the dowels. Get the laminate into the right position, then remove the dowels one by one from one end, gently pressing the laminate into position.

12 Once the sheet is down, ensure a good bond by hammering with a block of softwood over the entire surface. Pay special attention to the edges for a permanent bond. The edges can then be trimmed at a right angle to the face of the laminate and flush with the edge using a metal file.

The file must only be used pushing down on the laminate, never pulling up, as this may break the bond, which takes several days to reach its maximum strength. If you have access to one, a laminate trimmer or a router with a laminate trimming bit and pilot will save hours of work.

Repeat this with the other side if necessary. Also apply laminate to the exposed faces of the base unit. Where two faces of laminate meet, it is wise to file the joint at roughly 45° or 60° to remove the sharp edge. This will leave the typical dark edge line that is a feature of trimmed laminates. Once again, this can easily be done with a laminate trimming bit.

18 Fix the self-adhesive door-stops to the top shelf to soften the contact between table top and cabinet when the unit is closed. Also fit the cam-type sash lock to the top batten/cleat and the catch to the underside of the outer table edge. Check that it is in the correct position with the table up.

19 Fit lengths of the iron-on edge veneer to the front of the particle (chip) board shelves for a professional finish. This is applied with a household iron set on high – the adhesive on the edging will be melted. Finish the bond by running over the edging with a soft timber block while the adhesive is cooling. Then trim the edges flush with the top and bottom of each shelf.

20 The final major components needed to finish the unit are the doors. The right door is 524 mm wide x 1910 mm in height, and the left is 534 mm, with the leading edge rebated 10 mm to define the joint and to hide any slight irregularity that may result in the fitting.

21 Each door is fixed with three overlay hinges. These are semi-concealed and easy to install. The top and bottom hinges will need to be slightly let into the door to allow the hinge to sit flush with the top and bottom of the door. Cut an angled slot halfway down the door to accommodate the middle hinge. Each door will take one of one hand, and two of the other hand hinges.

22 Mark the position of the hinge screw holes on the door, and lightly predrill the screw hole. Similar predrilling should be done on the cabinet edge – this will ensure that the screws enter straight. It also helps to get the screws started through the laminate.

23 Fit the small magnetic catches to the top and bottom of the cabinet and fit the knobs to the doors. If desired, a power point can be added to the inside face of the cabinet above the laminated shelf.

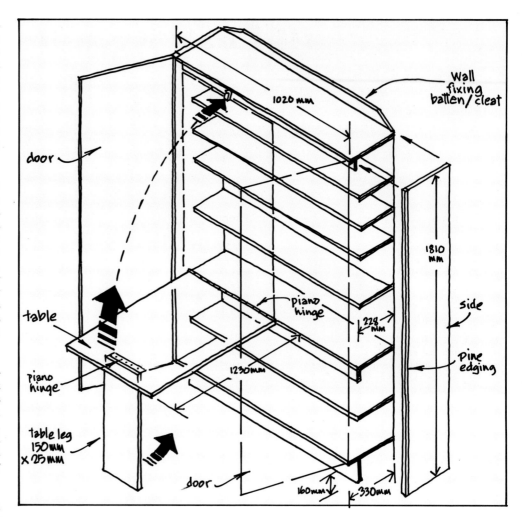

 ## Skill Class
Dowel joints

This type of joint is used to join pieces of timber together side by side to increase the overall width – such as may be necessary for timber shelves. Dowels can only be used if the timber is thicker than 12 mm – any less, and there is not enough room to insert the dowels. Dowelling is a simple and concealed method of making a strong edge joint.
❑ Once the joint is planed true, square pencil lines across the edges to mark the position of the dowels. Separate the timber and use a gauge from the face side of each board, set to half the timber thickness, to mark at each pencil line. The point of intersection is the position of the dowel centre.
❑ Bore holes for the dowels, standing at the end of the work to make sure the drill is perpendicular to the timber. Now slightly countersink the holes. Make sure that the dowel length is slightly shorter than the combined depth of the holes, with the ends bevelled. Finally, run a saw kerf along the dowel if not already grooved.

❑ To assemble the joint, put adhesive into the holes and glue onto the dowels, then knock the dowels into the holes in one of the timber pieces. Clean off any surplus adhesive and then add the other piece of timber and lightly cramp together.

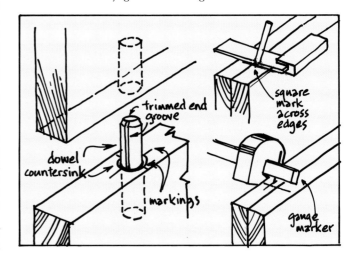

In Easy Reach

Designing to the correct dimensions for effective and comfortable use is a science in itself. It is called ergonomics. Today it is a fundamental part of designing the environments people work in.

When you start planning a project, you will already have a general idea of the size you want a structure to be and how it will fit in. Before you can make actual construction plans, you need to determine the exact dimensions of your project.

This is the science of anthropometry, which is concerned with the measurement of the human body. A lot of research has been carried out throughout the world to compile average body sizes and these measurements are used to achieve the correct relationship between people and their working environment. This means designing or selecting furniture and storage facilities that are best suited to your use.

The reason why kitchen worktops or benches are usually 900 mm high is because that height is best suited to most people when standing. The typical depth of 600 mm enables everything on the bench to be within reach. Tables and desks are usually set at 750 mm because that height suits the mean dimensions of the adult human body.

The accompanying dia-grams show average European dimensions. When you are planning to build something, use these dimensions as a guide.

When designing for storage shelves or fittings, allow the maximum dimensions for the items to be stored, such as large books and folders, computer disks or music tapes.

If you are designing a study desk, you may want to allow for a set of filing cabinets under it. These will vary in size so that you will need to check the actual dimensions.

It is likely that you will not have enough room for everything to be stored within convenient reach of the main work area. Decide which items you are going to need on a regular basis and place these close to the work level. Long-term storage, such as old reference books or files, can be stored higher up.

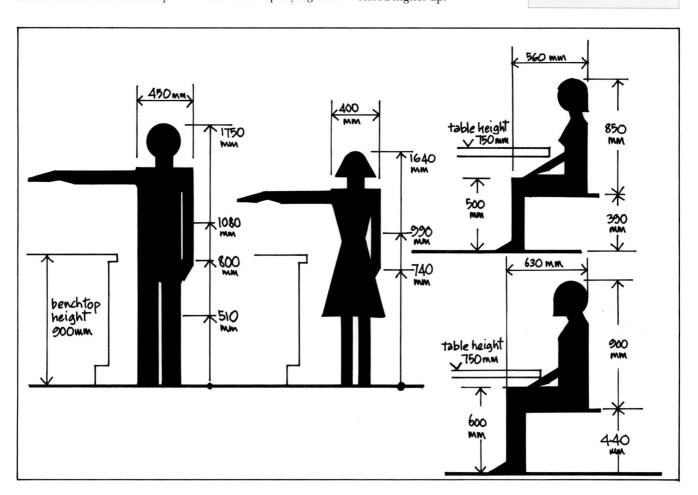

The cosy book-lined study of past generations is rapidly changing into the home office of today. Even if you just want a little office space for family records and financial matters – it pays to organise it properly to suit the job at hand.

HOME OFFICE

Although a 'study' conjures up a very different image from that of a 'home office', it is used for the same activities: paperwork, reading, study, peace and quiet, household accounts, correspondence, and so on. A home office, however, suggests something more streamlined and modern (and possibly even profitable!).

Efficient storage is an essential and integral part of a well-organised home office or study. Your work area needs to be thoughtfully planned around the type of work you do. For example, if you are involved with design and drawing work, you will need a lot of deep desk space, pin-up space on the walls and cardboard tubes for storage of drawing paper. Make a list of the items you use regularly when working. For example:
- ❏ pen and pencils
- ❏ paper and other stationery items
- ❏ telephone
- ❏ desk lamp
- ❏ calculator
- ❏ filing trays
- ❏ suspension (hanging) files
- ❏ typewriter/computer keyboard and screen
- ❏ waste-paper basket
- ❏ personal mementos
- ❏ reference books

Remember that items should be easy to locate, see and reach. Fitted coordinated storage units are neater than freestanding ones.

Office equipment

Today's hi-tech communication equipment – mobile telephones, answering machines, personal computers and printers, modems and facsimile machines – all allow home-based workers to communicate easily with clients or head office.

Consider the location of the equipment you will need, both now and in the future. Location of computers and peripheral equipment is important not only because of limitations on the length of leads from the computer and the printer, but also because of the large number of power and data leads which will hang about. One way to free-up your work surface is to install a duct at the back of the desk or clip the cables under the desk with holes in the top through which the cables can be drawn.

Don't forget the need for storing boxes of computer and photocopying paper and other bulk supplies.

Storage solutions

A home office may lack sufficient floor space to accommodate a large desk, or enough wall space to locate all the shelves and cupboards you need. Our Deskmate (Project 7) on page 51 and Window storage box (Project 8) on page 52 are simple and quick to make and can be finished to suit your office/study design.

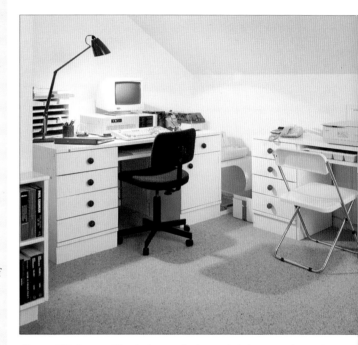

Above: This home office is the result of an attic/loft conversion and has everything in easy reach

Below: Study area in the den

IKEA

Props from FREEDOM

Clockwise from left:
A workspace for a small home business dealing in dried flowers and pot pourri; Hi-tech office furniture – smart and easy to adjust for changing storage needs; Small office area with a bookcase, desk and return; Desk accessories; Home office with a view

A home office is for paper work, concentration and private retreat, so locate it in the quietest part of your home.

Study and computer centre

The work area of your home office/study must be designed for working in comfort with everything in easy reach and at the right height.

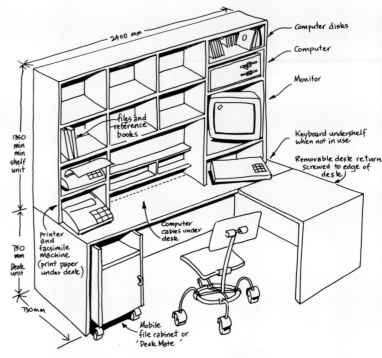

2400 mm

1350 min min shelf unit

750 mm Desk unit

750 mm

Computer disks

Computer

Monitor

files and reference books

Keyboard undershelf when not in use

Removable desk return screwed to edge of desk

Printer and facsimile machine (print paper under desk)

Computer cables under desk

Mobile file cabinet or 'Desk Mate'

LARGE COMPUTER AREA

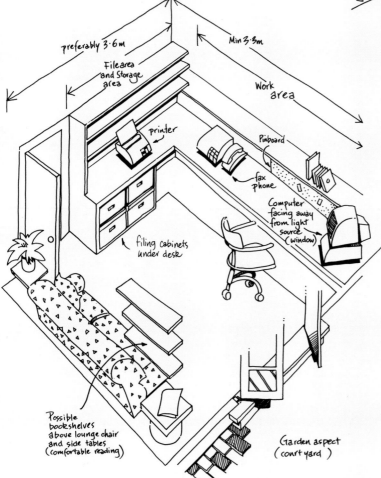

preferably 3.6m

Min 3.3m

File area and Storage area

Work area

printer

Pinboard

fax phone

Computer facing away from light source (window)

filing cabinets under desk

Possible bookshelves above lounge chair and side tables (comfortable reading)

Garden aspect (court yard)

HOME OFFICE PLAN

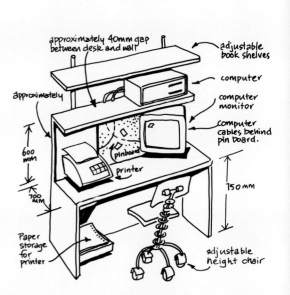

approximately 40mm gap between desk and wall

adjustable book shelves

computer

computer monitor

computer cables behind pin board.

approximately

600 mm

700 mm

pinboard

printer

150 mm

Paper storage for printer

adjustable height chair

SMALL COMPUTER CENTRE

Deskmate

A deskmate is a mobile storage cabinet which is stored out of the way under a desk and rolled out when needed.

There are a number of different configurations ranging from simple storage of paper, envelopes and a few files you may be working on, to a deskmate which can store a printer on the top with the paper feeding from the shelf at the back.

STEP BY STEP

1 Follow the cutting diagram for cutting out the panels. It is best to mark out one panel at a time and cut this out before cutting the next. This will ensure that you set the panels at the correct size. Remember the saying 'Measure twice, cut once'.

The side, bottom, middle and back panels should be cut first. Mark out the size of the panel, ensuring the sides are perpendicular to each other by using a try square. Use a timber batten/cleat as a guide for the power saw to run along. This will result in a much cleaner job. Measure your saw to find the distance from the guide fence to the side of the blade teeth. Mark this distance from the line you are to cut and temporarily fix the batten/cleat in position with small nails.

2 Fix these main panels with PVA adhesive and nails, checking that the panels are square as you proceed. Once these panels are nailed in place, fix screws as well, about 50 mm from corners and edges. Drill pilot holes smaller than the screw shaft and countersink the hole so that the end of the screw finishes below the face of the panels.

3 At this point you should check the dimensions for the remaining panels in case the first panels are a different size to the cutting diagram. This is particularly important for the door panel, which should be check-measured and cut after the main panels are fixed together. Fix the door hinges following the manufacturer's instructions. The hinges allow final adjustment of the door panel by turning grub screws on the face of the hinges.

4 All that remains is to fix the timber battens/cleats, aluminium angle and the castors to the bottom.

5 When the unit is complete, use a fine sandpaper to rub down the edges then under-coat. Leave to dry, following the instructions on the paint tin. Use an oil-based paint for the final coats (this will resist abrasions more easily). Paint two coats, sanding down with wet and dry sandpaper between coats.

TIP: Nailing provides a handy way to hold panels together while the adhesive sets and you drive the screws. But don't rely on nails alone for strength.

MATERIALS

ITEM	DIMENSIONS (mm)	QUANTITY
medium-density fibreboard (MDF)	2.4 m x 1.2 m x 12 thick	1 sheet
timber batten/cleat (DAR/PAR)	25 x 25	1
aluminium angle	25 x 25	1
PVA adhesive		
particle (chip) board screws		
25 mm twisted-shank nails		
hinges for particle (chip) board doors		2
castors		4
all-purpose undercoat and oil-based paint for finishing		

SPECIAL TOOLS
hand-saw and power saw
electric drill
hammer and screwdriver

TIME
Allow 4 hours to construct and another two days for the painting (one coat of undercoat and two finishing coats).

CUTTING SCHEDULE

ITEM	DIMENSIONS (mm)	QTY
A	606 x 540	2
B	440 x 272	1
C	440 x 528	1
D	440 x 606	1
E	440 x 320	1
F	436 x 320 (allows tolerance for fitting)	1
G (door)	462 x 436	1

Project 8

Window storage box

This very simple box with its hinged-top lid panels is ideal for storing items such as copier or computer paper, old job files and children's artistic endeavours.

The box used here is 2.4 m long to suit the standard length of MDF board, but could be shorter. The completed box can be positioned under a window and finished off with cushions, or placed anywhere in your office or study, depending on layout, so that it doubles as a piece of furniture.

STEP BY STEP

1 Follow the cutting diagram for cutting out the panels. Use a guide batten/cleat for the power saw, as described for Project 7 (Deskmate). Start by cutting out the front, back and two end panels together with the plywood base.

2 Apply adhesive to the edges of the panels and nail together. Once the side and end panels are nailed together, and before the adhesive has dried, glue and nail the base plywood panel in place with panel pins. Make sure that the corners are square before nailing the base in place. Now screw the panels near each corner.

3 Turn the partly completed box over and check-measure for the centre panel and top lid panels. Cut the centre panel and nail and screw in place. Fix the hinges to the lid panels and set in place.

4 All that remains is to sand down the edges of the panels, undercoat and finish.

TIP: Nailing provides a handy way to hold panels together while the adhesive sets and you drive the screws. But don't rely on nails alone for strength.

MATERIALS

ITEM	DIMENSIONS (mm)	QUANTITY
medium-density fibreboard (MDF)	2.4 x 1.2 x 16 thick	2 sheets
plywood	2.4 x 0.9 x 4 thick	1 sheet
PVA adhesive		
particle (chip) board screws		
25 mm twisted-shank nails		
panel pins		
hinges for particle (chip) board doors		8
all-purpose undercoat and oil-based paint for finishing		

SPECIAL TOOLS
handsaw and power saw
electric drill
hammer and screwdriver

TIME
Allow 6 hours to construct and another two days for the painting (one coat of undercoat and two finishing coats).

CUTTING SCHEDULE		
Item	Dimensions (mm)	Qty
A	2400 x 600 (cut into four)	1
B	2400 x 384	1
C	2400 x 384	1
D	568 x 384	2
E	568 x 384	1
Base	2400 x 600	

GREEN TIP

Paper recycling bin or box
One storage article that deserves the little space it takes up in every room or every second room is the paper recycling bin or box. It's not until you start re-cycling old newspapers, magazines and junk mail that you notice the vast quantity of paper waste created in an average week. It is quite staggering. Re-use your paper as much as possible before disposing of it. If your community does not yet have collection days or recycling depots, make a fuss until they start.

SKILL CLASS

MORTISE AND TENON

This joint is quite commonly used. It is used for joining timber together at right angles to each other, and basically consists of a recess (the mortise) in one piece and the tenon (cut to fit into the mortise) at the end of the other piece (see illustration).

PLAIN GLUED JOINTS

Where glue is to be relied on solely for the joint bond, the edges need to be accurately planed. Relying on cramps to close up gaps between the edges

of the timber is not enough.
❏ For a straight edge to the timber, use a long plane such as a jointing plane, which will give a straighter edge than a smoothing plane.
❏ The best method is to remove shavings from the middle until the plane ceases to cut, and then take a couple of shavings right through. In this way, the edge is first made slightly hollow, and then this is corrected when the final shavings are taken off. Generally, this method will work well for joints up to 900 mm long.

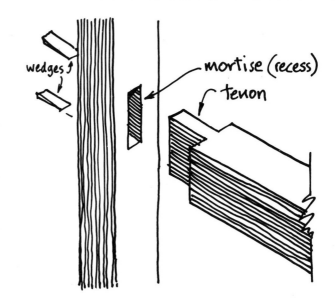

wedges
mortise (recess)
tenon

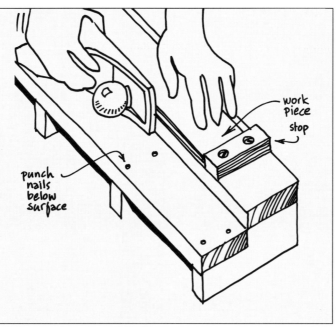

work piece stop

punch nails below surface

Making a shooting board

Use a shooting board with a hand plane for accurate planing work. Used with a jack or jointer plane, it is ideal for accurate planing of end grain or the edges of long thin panels. The shooting board consists of two boards, which guide the plane, and a stop, which holds the timber in place. The timber for the shooting board should be about 1 m long and made out of straight seasoned hardwood, although plywood will do. Glue and nail the boards to timber spacers and punch the nails when you have finished.

USING A HANDSAW

❏ When holding a saw, extend the index finger down the side of the handle – this provides some lateral restraint on the saw.

TIPSTRIP

NAILING NEAR EDGES OF TIMBER

Whenever nailing near the edge of a piece of timber, always drill a pilot hole for each nail slightly smaller in diameter than the nail. This will prevent splitting of the timber.

❏ When starting a cut, place your thumb as a guide beside the saw blade, which is on the waste side of the cutting line. Make the first few strokes backward, leaving the thumb against the blade until the cut is well under way.

USING A CIRCULAR SAW

The circular saw is generally used by all tradespeople for a variety of uses. It can be used for crosscutting and ripcutting as well as rebating and grooving, by adjusting the blade depth.
❏ Make sure that the saw motor is not overloaded. The

saw blade should be running at full speed before it comes into contact with the timber.
❏ Never start the motor when the blade is in contact with timber.
❏ When in use, ease the saw forward slowly and smoothly without too much forward pressure, which will strain the motor.
❏ If the motor speed drops, ease back and let the motor speed come back up before continuing.
❏ Always set the saw blade so that its teeth just penetrate the other side of the timber.

TIPSTRIP

SMOOTH-CUTTING TIMBER

When timber is cut with a saw it will leave a slightly rough edge. The following method of cutting timber with a sharp edge is commonly used in cabinet joints.
❏ After marking the cut, scribe the mark line with a sharp chisel several times to make an incision in the timber face.
❏ Next, use the chisel to cut a small sloping groove on the waste side of the cut – this groove will provide a channel in which the saw can run.
Note: This method will give you an accurate cut and a sharp edge.

❏ If you are cutting large panels of timber or sheets of particle (chip) board, use a timber batten/cleat, or a narrow offcut as a guide for the edge of the power saw to run along. This will give a straight edge and a much cleaner job.
    Measure your saw to find the distance from the edge of the sole plate to the side of the blade teeth. Mark this distance from the line you are to cut and temporarily fix the batten/cleat in position with small nails or clamps.

When you next look around your home thinking that you couldn't swing a cat let alone put away your record collection, think again. Even the smallest studio flat has storage potential. You can make your tiny corner of the city a more spacious and pleasant place to live.

TIGHT CORNERS

Finding somewhere reasonably central at a price you can afford, especially if you are single, often means sacrificing the luxury of space. This usually means living in a one-bedroom flat or a studio apartment where storage space and the most efficient use of your living space is of paramount importance. Not for you the convenience of the loft space where those unused belongings lurk out of sight and out of mind. What you have, you use – and it has to be on hand, but not under your feet.

Kitchen

Unless you're very lucky, the one room in the house where you are very unlikely to have a lot of space to spare is the kitchen. Think in terms of the room's volume and not the floor area. If you're leading a busy lifestyle, there are going to be things you need every day and those things that you don't – make sure everyday items are easily accessible.

❏ Cupboards and shelves should be built up to the ceiling, allowing work areas to be placed at a convenient height for food preparation.

❏ Even in a very tight space, storage can still be used as a decorative feature. An old-fashioned dresser will add character to your kitchen and is an excellent way to show off your crockery and glassware.

❏ Every wall space is a potential storage area – attach a mesh rack to the wall and use hooks to hang bulky items such as ladles and colanders; hang pots and pans from a sturdy ceiling rack; a wall-mounted spice rack above your worktop may do wonders for your cooking! Racks and hooks can also be used in a small hallway to hang up coats, scarves, hats and umbrellas.

❏ Another storage idea that can grow as you need it is a modular vegetable rack – fill it with all your favourites!

❏ Shelving should be deep enough to store large casseroles and the like – but not so deep that you lose things!

❏ Sharp kitchen knives can be stuck to the wall using a magnetic knife rack – make sure it is safely located away from little fingers!

Bathroom

How many times have you felt your bathroom has been invaded by the shampoo bottles from outer space? You know what it's like – all those bottles of shampoo, last year's suntan lotion and a doctor's cabinet of 'flu remedies that you're loath to chuck out!

❏ Install a shelf above the bath (along its length) or, alternatively, install several smaller shelves above the bath taps. Another solution is to have small shelves fitted into the angle of two walls.

❏ A multi-tiered trolley for bathtime essentials is movable and adaptable.

❏ Hooks are another quick-fix solution for hanging towels, clothes and pot plants.

Above: Entrance/hallway
Right: Office/study in a cupboard

This small but well-designed inner-city apartment is full of clever, space-saving storage solutions.

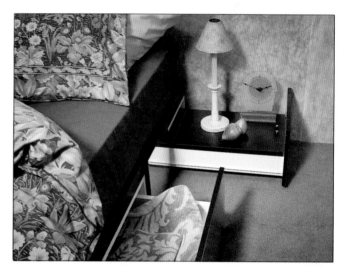

Clockwise from top left: Pull-out drawers under window seating in living area; Compact kitchen; Pull-out bedside table and drawers in bedroom; Bedroom wall cabinets; Floor to ceiling wardrobe and shelving system; Bathroom

Styling: Michelle Gorry
Graheme McIntosh, Interior Design Consultant

Props courtesy of: Private Collection, Made Where; Sandy de Beyer; Les Olivades; Made in Japan; In Residence; Version; The Annexe; The Dressing Room; Mary Lou's Linen and Bathroom Shoppe

Multipurpose mezzanine

The living room is often the most important room in a flat and in many cases also doubles up as a bedroom. Put yourself up on the shelf by building a mezzanine floor! This idea requires a fairly large room with highish ceilings. A mezzanine is easy and cheap to build, can make a very attractive feature and, most importantly, can be a real selling point when you decide to sell. It is quite simply the most space-saving thing you could hope to have – even the steps up to it form an eye-catching tiered storage space perfect for storing all your documents and files in attractive stackable boxes. Underneath can become a cosy spot to place the sofa or a desk. Otherwise you can devote the whole space to storage – it is the ideal place to put your hi-fi, television and video and the like.

Dual-purpose bed

Of course, not everyone has the possibility of building a mezzanine, so now is the time to start thinking about a dual-purpose sofa bed or divan. It's a worthwhile investment –

QUICK-FIX PROJECT
Stackable cane suitcases
What could be more attractively practical than a stack of cane suitcases? These were purchased at a low-price home-decorating chain store, then painted inside and out with gloss spray paint.
To dress up your suitcases, simply line the lid base and inner lower part of each with polyester batting, gluing the edges to secure. Cover the wadding again with fabric pieces, turning under

after all, there's no point having more space to move around in if you can't even get up in the morning! Divan drawers are excellent for storing spare blankets and out-of-season clothes.

Revamping junk

❑ Do up a second-hand blanket box – it can double as a coffee or bedside table or sit at the end of your bed.

the outer edges of fabric to neaten. Glue to secure. Glue braid over edges, and trim as you wish. The fabric lining will mean that the suitcases remain dust free and insect-proof, and

can be used to store woollens and household linen. Just for good measure, place some pot pourri sachets and mothballs in the bottom.

❑ Revamp an old wardrobe or cupboard and put shelves inside to double your storage space. Install a shoe rack and wire baskets in the bottom too.

Wall-to-wall shelving

The classic solution for storage problems is wall-to-wall shelving. Break up the monotony with recesses for your collectables, ornaments and pot plants. The shelves can be of different sizes and strengths according to what you want to store on them.

Freestanding pluses

Freestanding storage units such as desks and worktops, drawers and cupboards can be used as room dividers or as island units. One plus is that you can rearrange the room whenever you feel like a change, or take the units with you when you move on. Built-in cupboards can be tailored to suit your needs but they *are* permanent fixtures – you'll need to weigh up the pros and cons of fixed versus freestanding storage units.

Divan bed in a teenager's sitting room

Cane chests

Fabric pouches for general storage

Under-the-bed storage drawer

Children always seem to need more storage than anyone else in the home! Although it's worth remembering that storage alone doesn't tidy the room. This portable drawer on castors slides neatly away into whatever space is available.

The measurements given for this project may not suit the space you have under your bed. Adapt the design and measure for your own sizes, remembering to consider the height of the castors in the overall height. You may decide to make two smaller boxes instead of one large box.

STEP BY STEP

1 Cut all pieces to precise sizes required.

2 Glue and nail front to sides.

3 Glue and nail back to sides.

4 Glue and nail supports between front and back at each side and one in the middle, level with lower edges so the 70 mm dimension is horizontal.

5 Nail through side panels into supports.

6 Screw castors onto supports at each corner so that they do not swivel beyond the outer edges of the drawer.

7 Cut base to specified size and drop into frame.

MATERIALS

ITEM	DIMENSIONS (mm)	QUANTITY
front and back, softwood DAR (PAR)	1220 x 240 x 20 thick	2
sides, softwood DAR (PAR)	765 x 240 x 20 thick	2
supports, softwood DAR (PAR)	765 x 70 x 20 thick	3
base, ply or softwood DAR (PAR)	1180 x 765 x 15 thick	1
castors and screws as required		2 pairs
panel pins		
PVA adhesive		

SPECIAL TOOLS
saw

TIME
2-3 hours

QUICK-FIX PROJECT
Blanket box
This once shabby old toy box has been transformed into a very attractive blanket box for storage purposes. It has been lined and covered with medium thickness quilter's wadding, then the fabric of our choice. All pieces were cut to size, allowing for turn-unders and overlaps. The edges were stapled, glued or held with decorative upholstery tacks. Woven braid covers some overlapped areas inside, for example where the lining meets the exterior fabric. A length of fine chain with an eyehook (screweye) at each end attaches the lid to the inside of the box, and prevents it flipping open too far. New handles were added.

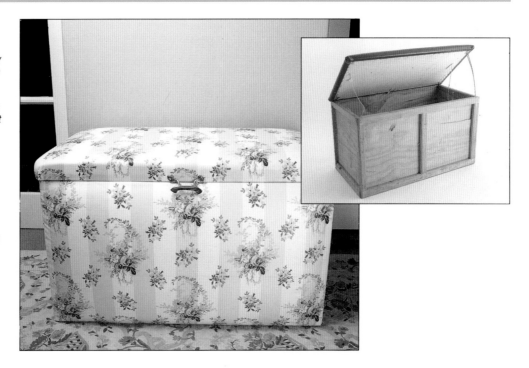

For an area that is used several times a week and is always hard at work to keep you looking your best, the laundry is often sadly neglected. Pay it a little attention, too, and solve those washday blues at the same time.

WASHDAY BLUES

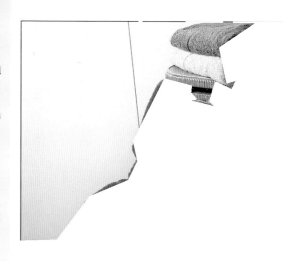

To get the most space and ease out of your laundry, first consider its layout and be critical about its shortcomings. Many householders have no choice but to incorporate the laundry into the bathroom or kitchen, so the laundry basket, peg bag, sink unit, bucket, washing machine, dryer, detergents and all the rest of it has to be fitted in as unobtrusively as possible. Your laundry may even be positioned in a narrow passageway or back corner. Don't despair – well-thought-out planning doesn't require a lot of space.

If your appliances rest on the floor, take full advantage of any unused wall space above by fixing a full-length cupboard along the wall. The deeper the better – you can always use the extra room for safe storage of cleaning solutions and spare light bulbs. By building an enclosed cupboard around your washing machine and dryer you can hide them away while at the same time creating valuable worktop space for folding and sorting.

If you have enough room, also allow space for an airing cupboard – it will prove to be an invaluable in-between storage area. A fold-away ironing board attached to the wall also saves space and eliminates the often awkward storage of a traditional freestanding one. Don't forget about stackable wire baskets, racks and hooks – they take up very little room

and provide handy extra storage.

Stacking your front-loading washing machine and dryer will help create immediate space (see Project 10, Laundry in a cupboard on page 60). If possible, try to leave some room between them for a pull-out shelf to rest your laundry basket on, or for folding clothes. Stacking your appliances may also free you of space to build a tall side-cupboard, which is sometimes easier to access than the high mounted type of cupboard. Shallow, wire pull-drawers are excellent for storing sewing utensils for on-the-spot repairs. Install a wire rack or hanging rails for hanging ironed shirts and other clothes.

If space isn't a problem, include built-in bins for dirty clothes so that the whites can be separated from the coloureds. Two more bins for clean clothes will complete the set, one for clothes which need to be folded and the other for those to be ironed. A stylish choice of cane baskets can also be a help here. Cane baskets last virtually forever and are highly portable and environmentally friendly.

If your laundry is confined to a small, awkward space, why not hide your appliances behind bifold doors, louvres, Roman blinds or curtains? Or convert space in an alcove or under a stairway into a new laundry.

Just make sure you take into account electrical outlets

Clockwise from top:
From house to line – a colourful set of cane baskets and a pegbag are all you need;
Foldaway ironing centre;
Laundry behind bifold doors;
Laundry shelving – the wall has been opened up and narrow shelves fitted in between noggings

Whitegoods supplied by Hoover

and the surrounding floor covering (carpets do not sit well with washing spills). With small laundries try and keep things sleek and simple – the less cluttered it is the more organised you'll feel.

If you are lucky enough to have a small room devoted to it or have space to spare, think about turning your laundry into a multipurpose utility room packed with convenience. Wouldn't it be nice to have a complete sewing and mending centre close at hand? Or a room you can count on for 101 tasks, from polishing your shoes or silver to fixing that broken lamp?

Transforming your laundry can often be as simple as installing additional cupboards and shelving where space permits. See-through wire baskets, too, are readily found and slide easily under countertops. Drying racks can double as an extra space for ironed clothes. Use the worktop as a desk and sewing area, positioned by a sunny window if possible. Sewing enthusiasts will appreciate the convenience of having a walled pegboard to keep thread and scissors.

With so many practical storage options, it's easy to get carried away. But don't forget about the finishing touches. A friendly, warm colour scheme and comfortable chair or stool will make all the difference in turning your utility room into an area you'll enjoy using.

Clockwise from top: Utility room – an area for soiled clothes and clothes drying, mending/ sewing centre ; Handy attachment for drying smalls and delicates; Detail of mending/ sewing centre showing drawers for storage of sewing materials and a self-charging vacuum for picking up stray threads

The value of a good utility room has to be experienced to be appreciated: it is an area set aside for 101 different jobs.

Laundry in a cupboard

Although this project was built in a specific location, it incorporates many options and can easily be modified to suit individual needs and available space.

In this case, a laundry, including the washing machine, a dryer, a laundry tub/sink and the dirty clothes basket, was installed in one section of a large built-in area (to a depth of 850 mm) in the family room. The front of the built-in has a series of off-the-shelf, floor-to-ceiling wardrobe doors hinged as pairs. Choose ready-made doors in the closest size and adapt frame sizes to suit. The dryer was mounted over the washing machine on its own support provision. Inside, three shelves were installed adjacent to and above the dryer.

MATERIALS

ITEM	DIMENSIONS (mm)	QUANTITY
doors	2340 x 620 x 35 thick	2
door frames (not rebated)	75 x 38	2 (2.4 m) 1 (1.5 m)
hinges	75 butt	6
brackets	125 x 150 100 x 125	4 4
particle (chip) board	2440 x 1220 x 15 thick 25 x 25	offcuts or 1 sheet
battens/cleats, softwood (DAR/PAR)		1 length (3.6 m)
vents to suit		2 exterior 2 interior
washing machine stop cocks		1 set
washing machine standpipe		1 set
ceramic tiles, wall tiling adhesive and grout		3 sq m
oil-based sealer and water-based paint to finish		

SPECIAL TOOLS
tile cutter and grouting tool
router

TIME
Approximately two weekends

STEP BY STEP

1 Measure up the area accurately, including ceiling height, depth of cupboard and location of any power points. Note sizes of facilities to be built in.
In this project:
❏ washing machine (620 mm wide x 720 mm needed from rear wall x 1100 mm high)

❏ dryer (620 mm wide x 520 mm deep x 720 mm high)

❏ laundry tub/sink (680 mm wide x 420 mm deep x 890 mm high)

Make a sketch of the project including sizes and notes as to what will happen where.

2 Organise to have a plumber install hot and cold water supply as well as adequate drainage for both the automatic washing machine and the tub/sink.

3 Have the power point changed to a double power outlet that can take the load of both the washing machine and the dryer operating simultaneously. If you want lighting installed, this can be done at the same time. A further requirement if operating a dryer is to provide ventilation to the outside of the wall to expel humidity.

4 Once all the plumbing and wiring have been installed, the walls can be made good. (In this case, the right and rear walls were plastered and simply needed filling where the chasing was done, to get back to a good surface.)

5 Install two high vents to allow good air flow through the space, especially when the dryer is being used. Vents can be installed by removing three bricks from the exterior of the house. This is most easily done by drilling a series of closely spaced holes into the mortar. Use a hammer drill set on low speed with a 10 mm tungsten carbide masonry bit. The remaining mortar can be removed with a plugging chisel. Take care to prevent debris from falling into the wall cavity.

6 Cut a similar hole inside to coincide with the outside. The outside can then have a terra-

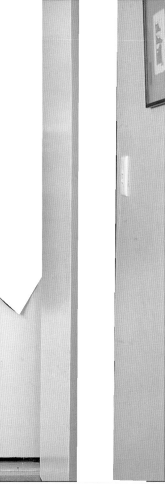

cotta vent/airbrick to match the brickwork, or perhaps better still a brass mesh vent or plastic-coated airbrick, which allows good air circulation. If it is an exposed wall, a hooded vent may be required. Set the vent/airbrick in place using a mortar mix to match the colour of the exterior – use a 1:1:6 cement, lime and sand mix. Use two half bricks to fill in around the vents. Install plaster vents with flyscreens on the inside, using a cornice cement, and fill to finish neatly to the internal render.

7 If you are required to have power ventilation, arrange to install a power point high on the wall – this will make it easier for you to install a plug-in type extractor fan. Once again, a large hole will have to be made in the brick and the internal skin to fit the fan. Most through-wall fans are made with an outside cowling that will shed water, and have an integral duct that is adaptable to most common wall thicknesses. There are also various ducting kits available. When in place, cut the bricks around the outside to

cover the installation and cement them in place. The cowling will cover most of the ragged edges.

8 It is important to install the shelving before the doors, as the framing and doors will only hinder working in a tight space. The shelves are all made of 15 mm particle (chip) board. Cut the first shelf (top) to 1615 mm x 760 mm. This shelf is full width at 1615 mm and is positioned at a height of 2110 mm from the floor and held up by battens/cleats screwed to the walls. Masonry walls will have to be plugged. This involves predrilling with a masonry bit, inserting a plastic plug and then screwing into that. The timber should also be primed before installation for maximum protection in case of high humidity in the laundry. As this shelf is spanning a distance greater than 1600 mm across the front, otherwise unsupported, a structural member (or beam) needs to be installed to ensure the shelf does not sag. This is best done with a similar length of 75 mm x 25 mm timber, glued and screwed on edge to the underside of the

shelf with 50 mm x No. 8 gauge screws. The shelf and lintel should be primed ready for painting.

9 Cut the second shelf smaller, 980 mm wide by 250 mm deep, with a return coming out the left-hand side, 780 mm x 250 mm. Fix the shelf at 1810 mm from the floor on 150 mm x 125 mm brackets fixed to the wall by screwing as before. Once again, the shelf should then be primed. The third shelf is the smallest at 980 mm wide and 150 mm deep, with a return of 780 mm out of the left wall. Fix the shelf 1510 mm from the floor on 100 mm x 125 mm brackets.

10 The opening to the laundry cupboard is defined by a light timber casing with a horizontal timber member, which comes down about 110 mm from the ceiling, installed over the top of the doors. Finish this either with some leftover particle (chip) board (painted), or plasterboard. A 90 mm plain cornice can then be installed to finish the built-in laundry to the ceiling.

11 The door frames are rebated 12 mm deep to receive the doors. The width of the rebate must be at least equal to the thickness of the door, plus 3 mm for clearance. The frames are made up as a set: the vertical side frames and the top frame. They are made up with a temporary diagonal brace and spacer at the bottom to maintain the correct width. The frame is nailed together before installation.

12 The door frames can now be prepared. The length of the side frame is set out to the height of the door plus top and bottom clearance. Top clearance is 2 mm and bottom clearance 10 mm. The width is set out as the width of the two doors plus 5 mm to allow for clearances. In this case, mark 1245 mm centrally onto the top frame, and square across. Line up short piece of frame material to the rebate, and mark the top frame each side for the width of the housing. This can then be cut to size, and the housing cut with a saw and chisel. Also cut a bottom brace and nail together the jambs, holding them square. A bottom

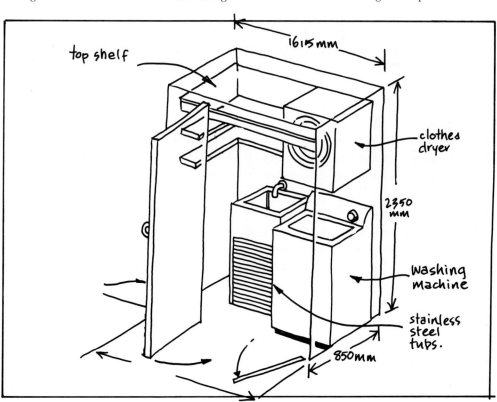

spreader, fitting 1245 mm exactly between the rebates, may help.

13 Check the floor across the opening for level. It normally would be level – if it is out then that amount will have to be cut from the bottom of the appropriate side frame to compensate. The top frame should always be level.

14 Stand the frames in the opening and lightly drive a small wedge directly over the side frames to hold in place. Make sure the frames are plumb, and then pack between the light timber casing and one frame near the bottom (suitable packing includes offcuts of plywood or hardboard) and nail the frame to the stud. Continue packing and nailing that frame at the top and up the sides, making sure it remains straight and plumb. Repeat this on the other frame, making sure the width between the rebates remains constant. Don't nail the top frame to the house. When fixed, remove spreader and brace.

15 The doors will be held with ordinary steel butt hinges. Before fitting the door, give both the bottom and top edges a good coat of primer and/or undercoat to seal them – this protects the door against delamination.

Stand one door in the opening and make sure it fits with adequate clearance. For a good tight fit, the side of the

door that is not fixed to the jamb may need to be bevelled slightly so that it will clear the neighbouring door when closing. Stand the door in the opening and use a spacer at the top for the right clearance, and then wedge underneath to hold the door in place. The hinges are fitted 150 mm down from the top and 200 mm up from the bottom, and one half way. Mark the position and size of the hinges on the jamb and the door using the hinge as a template. Use a sharp chisel to check out/recess the door and the jamb for the hinge, and fix the hinge flap to the door with two screws. It is a good idea to drill a small pilot hole for the screws, to make sure they go in squarely. Fit the other flap into the check-out on the jamb, and screw in securely. Make sure the door works properly without any hindrance before putting in all the screws. Make any necessary minor adjustments then insert the remaining screws.

Repeat this process for the other door.

16 The entire interior can now be painted. It is suggested that the walls first be cleaned down with sugar soap or similar, and then prepared using a universal oil-based sealer. This can then be coated with a water-based paint for an easy-care surface.

17 The doors and shelves should be painted with an oil-based system as oil-based paints have a better abrasion resist-

ance, and are also easier to clean. Undercoat the doors and shelves, and then apply two coats of finish over the top, sanding lightly between coats.

18 Have a plumber install the tub/sink and secure it to the wall in the correct position, allowing room for the washing machine. The tiling can then be done (up to a height of 1365 mm) around the washing machine and tub/sink and over the upturned lip of the bowl. Install the tiles in a thin bed of wall tiling adhesive, applied with a 4.5 mm notched trowel as in the manufacturer's instructions. Allow 24 hours for

Laundry in a cupboard – behind closed doors

the tiles to set then fill the joints with grout so that they shed water more effectively.

19 For the finishing touches fit selected knobs to the doors, and top and bottom catches to hold the doors shut. When this is done you can connect the washing machine, and hang the dryer on its supports.

SKILL CLASS
Housed joints

This joint is used mainly for fixing shelves to the vertical divisions. In the simplest type, the groove is taken right across the timber where it is exposed at both edges. A stopped housed joint entails stopping the housing from the face of the timber so that it is concealed when put together.
❏ To make a simple housed joint, mark the position of the joint deeply with a sharp chisel or knife and square, with two

lines equal to the depth of the shelf thickness.
❏ On the groove side of each line, cut a sloping channel with a chisel – this provides a guide for cutting with a tenon saw.
❏ Remove the waste timber in the groove with a chisel and then finish off with a hand router. Alternatively, all the waste can be removed with an electric router. The router ensures that the depth of the housing is constant.

GREEN TIP
❏ **Shop around.** Check the labels on different appliances for energy consumption levels. Buy an appliance low in energy use. Also ask about replacement parts and servicing – you want to get as many years use out of the appliance as possible.
❏ Buy equipment that suits your needs. If there are only two of you, buy a small washing machine and dryer. A large family will need more heavy-duty appliances to last the distance.
❏ Choice matters. Appliances with a range of settings are more versatile – for example, washing machines with a half-load option or a short cycle for the not-so-dirty wash.

Bathrooms are common storage trouble spots that seem to get very messy, very quickly. These days there are lots of bright ideas for bathroom storage that utilise every bit of available space.

BATHROOMS

Building a vanity unit around a pedestal basin will help disguise any unsightly pipework while creating extra shelf and cupboard space. Lining the area inside with waterproof shelving paper will help to guard against moisture and possible water leaks. Plastic baskets are readily available and are good for keeping various bathroom items such as stray plasters and razor blades. When choosing a basin, look for one that has an extra wide rim and, of course, recesses for soap. Pick the one as large as your basin space will accommodate.

Mirrored medicine cabinets are a time-favoured bathroom accoutrement, and with good reason. Positioned above the basin they provide easy reach for everyday toiletries and medicines, which are neatly hidden away. Open shelves are another option. Painted wood or melamine-coated particle (chip) board are a sensible choice of material, and while glass is an attractive alternative it must be forever wiped and kept clean. Plastic-coated wire-rack units are a good, economical shelving solution, and work particularly well in a smaller bathroom where heavy wood cupboards may be too overpowering. Whatever cupboards or shelving units you choose, make sure that fragile bottles are not where they can fall and break and that all medicines, detergents and poisons are either locked up or kept well out of the reach of children.

Make the most of generous bathtub rims by keeping soap dishes, shampoos, or a stack of folded handtowels along the surface. Bathtubs come in a reasonable selection of colours, shapes and sizes – if you opt for a larger, oversized tub, remember that it will be more costly to fill. In terms of space, freestanding tubs make little difference, and traditional cast iron ones can look quite charming in a more rustic-looking bathroom.

More economical than baths, showers can be bought as ready-made cubicles, custom-built, or incorporated into your existing bath. Ready-made cubicles come in a variety of styles, and some come with built-in towel racks and shampoo shelves. A better idea might be a custom-built tiled alcove. Just make sure you include a good shower curtain or glass/plastic screen. If you integrate your bath and shower, be sure you have a flat-bottomed bath (the wider the better) and add nonslip mats to the surface.

Invest some time and take pride in your bathroom's decor. A visit to your local bathroom showroom will give you an array of ideas on bathroom design, fittings and accessories. Soap dishes, towel rails, toothbrush-holders, waste bins and laundry baskets can be

Clockwise from top: Wall cabinets and cabinets under vanity; Heated towel rack; Wire basket for towel storage; Toiletries organiser drawer

Styling: Michelle Gorry   Mary Lou's Linen and Bathroom Shoppe

Project 11

Towel rack

This easy-to-make towel rack is one simple but effective storage solution for your bathroom.

STEP BY STEP

1 Cut out the particle (chip) board sides. Mark and then cut out the semicircular curve at the end of each side piece (each curve should have a 100 mm radius) using a jigsaw.

2 Apply iron-on edging strip to sides.

3 Measure up, mark out and drill holes for the dowel rails. Before drilling laminate you should punch a starting point with a centre punch. Drill, glue and screw the four lengths of dowel in place as indicated (see illustration), using screw caps to conceal the screw heads.

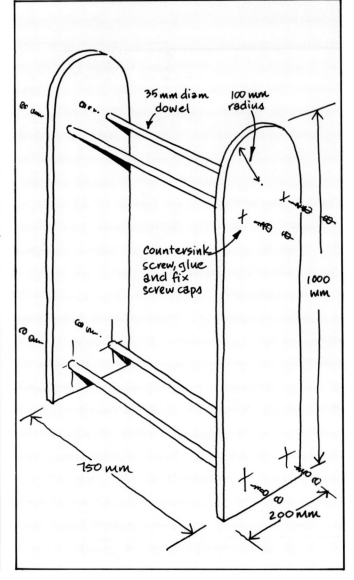

MATERIALS		
ITEM	DIMENSIONS (mm)	QUANTITY
plastic-laminated particle (chip) board for sides	1000 x 200 x 16 thick	2 sheets
dowel (rails)	750 x 35 diameter	4 lengths
iron-on edging strip	to cover 16 mm edge	5 m
screws		8
screw caps		8
waterproof adhesive		

SPECIAL TOOLS
jigsaw
electric drill

TIME
One or two days

practical as well as adding a nice finishing touch. Introduce an accent colour and buy your accessories in a coordinating range. Towel and magazine racks are also a useful addition, and can create lots of storage room. Mirrors are ideal for a smaller bathroom as they create the illusion of spaciousness.

Bathroom shelves

There is usually little call for extensive storage in bathrooms other than a place to hide the extra shampoo, cleaners and soaps. If you have a vanity unit this may well be adequate, but if you simply have a pedestal basin, you may wish to install a couple of small shelves underneath, cut to fit around the pedestal, with a little curtain across the front to hide the contents. This is easily done with a small rail of chrome or stainless steel tube made up to approximate the shape of the basin and screwed to the wall. The curtain, or curtain rings, can then be fed onto this and be opened and closed as with normal curtains.

Shelving with pull-down laundry cupboard in en suite

Bathside trolley

**Relax in the bath after a long day
with everything to hand on your
own bathside trolley.**

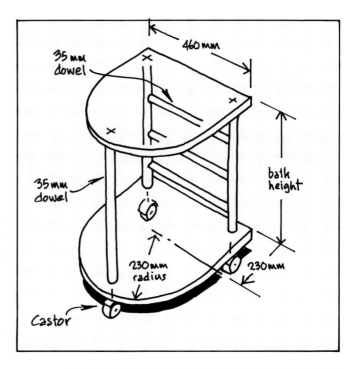

STEP BY STEP

1 Mark out then cut two semicircular shapes on each piece of 16 mm plastic-laminated particle (chip) board using a jigsaw. Each curve should have a 230 mm radius and an additional 230 mm depth at the straight edges.

2 Cover the exposed end-grain edges with iron-on edging strip.

3 Cut the three 35 mm dowels to match the height of your bath, taking into account the height of the castors and the two semicircular shelves.

4 Mark out, drill and insert three 400 mm lengths of 25 mm dowel horizontally to a depth of 20 mm between two of the 35 mm dowels to make the back leg structure.

5 Mark out, drill and insert screws through the two shelves into the ends of the three dowels. To conceal their heads in the top shelf of the trolley, use white sleeves and screw caps. Fit the conical sleeve over the screw when inserting and clipping the cap in place, after you have driven the screw home.

6 Screw the castors in place.

MATERIALS

ITEM	DIMENSIONS (mm)	QUANTITY
plastic-laminated particle (chip) board for shelves	460 x 460 x 16 thick	2 sheets
dowel (for legs)	35	3
dowel (for rails)	400 x 25	3
iron-on edging strip		
50 mm particle (chip) board screws		
conical white sleeves and screw caps		
castors		2 pairs

SPECIAL TOOLS
jigsaw
electric drill

TIME
One day

Wall (mirrored) cabinets and cupboards under vanity and full length of wall

Bedrooms seem to thrive on clutter! The good news is that a little creativity can go a long way. There are numerous things you can do to create more storage space and make for a more comfortable environment in the process.

BEDROOMS

The area around the bed holds several storage possibilities. A bedside table is a must; make sure you have plenty of room for an alarm clock, reading lamp, books and a telephone if you have a bedroom extension. Fabric draped over an old side-table is a quick and economical way to create a bedside table. It may, however, be worth your while to fully utilise the space below in the form of a low-lying bookcase, particularly if you're an avid reader.

Bedheads bring an attractive element to an otherwise little-used area of potential space behind the bed. You can buy several variations of modular units, and most come with matching bedside tables and frames. For the DIY enthusiast, bedheads can also be custom-made to match your specific requirements. Whatever you choose, remember to consider your lighting needs. Overhead and track lighting can add another dimension to your decor while freeing potential space. Adjustable and reading lights are practical choices for a bedside table because they occupy less space than traditional lamps.

And don't forget about the space under the bed. Retrieve those lost tennis shoes, and utilise the area to store out-of-season belongings using stackable boxes (hat, blanket and even shoe boxes). Bed frames with pull-out drawers are ideal, but empty suitcases can also do the same job. Storage trays on wheels are another good idea and let you get at your clothes easily (see Project 9, page 57). If you have some space at the foot of your bed, an old wooden chest or tin trunk can find a home here easily and create lots of storage space.

To get the most out of freestanding wardrobes, try installing hooks or tie/scarf racks inside the doors. The real advantage with freestanding furniture is its portability – it can be moved around as you wish to suit your changing needs and circumstances.

Built-ins are perfect for awkward or unused spaces. They can be expensive, but perhaps well worth the investment, renovation time or storage space saved. A good idea to try: with the bed across the corner, build a triangular-shaped cupboard behind it to store infrequently used items. Build adjoining bedside tables along the same angle as the bed, and continue (if desired) with a two-tiered shelf of the same height along the walls. Or try a built-in couch with storage space incorporated secretly underneath. The possibilities are endless, but remember to keep built-ins as simple as possible and neutral in colour to match the walls.

If you are blessed with walk-in cupboard space, consider adding a built-in wardrobe.

FREEDOM

Stack 'N' Store, Woollen jumpers from Benetton

Above: Tie/belt rack
Right: Wardrobe with stackable wire baskets
Below: Natural-finish trundle bed and bookshelves

Built-in cupboards and drawers can be custom-made to suit your needs.

FREEDOM

To 'customise' storage units, handles can be changed, doors can be painted or replaced with mirrored ones to increase the feeling of light and space.

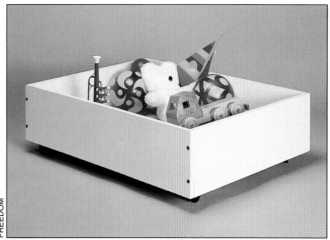

FREEDOM

Clockwise from top right: Toy box on wheels for under-the-bed storage; Floor to ceiling cabinets; Bright, portable and stackable storage; Robe savers; Built-in wardrobe

IKEA

Project 13

Handbag tidy

Always losing your handbag under a pile of clothes? Instead, why not put it away in your own handbag tidy?

STEP BY STEP

1 With right sides facing, stitch front and back print fabric panels together along top short edges. Press seam open. Repeat for plain fabric (lining) panels.

2 With right sides facing, stitch print and plain fabric panels together down long sides. Turn to right side. Press.

3 With print side uppermost, fold over hanger at seam line between front and back panels. Pin through all thicknesses and stitch from side to side 4 cm down from fold, to enclose hanger bar.

4 With right sides facing, stitch front and back print fabric panels together along bottom short edges. Press seam open. Turn to right side. Press matching plain fabric lining seams under 1 cm and slipstitch together to finish.

5 Mark four sections 48 cm deep on the front panel and four sections 30 cm deep on the back panel. Pin through all thicknesses matching marked lines and stitch from side to side to form four open-sided pockets.

MATERIALS

ITEM	QUANTITY
115 cm wide print cotton fabric	2 m
115 cm wide plain cotton fabric	2 m
coathanger	1

PATTERN

Cut one rectangle of print fabric 198 cm x 42 cm and one rectangle of plain fabric 198 cm x 42 cm for front panel. Cut one rectangle of print fabric 126 cm x 42 cm and one rectangle of plain fabric 126 cm x 42 cm for back panel. 1 cm seams allowed.

IKEA

Simple storage for the nursery

Remember to assess your storage needs first, then plan, build or buy accordingly. Start by asking yourself a few pertinent questions. Do you prefer your clothes folded or hung up? Just how long is your longest dress or pair of trousers? Maybe you want to include a space for jewellery, perfume and toiletries. Be sure to take into account your height so that objects are not out of reach.

A few more things to remember: cubby holes are the best way to store folded articles of clothing. If you choose drawers, it's a good idea to include several shallow ones as well as a variation of depths. Wire storage units are good because you can see what's inside them. Clear perspex on sliding drawers may cost a bit more, but is worth the investment, particularly if you have a lot of clothes. And when buying or building a wardrobe, remember that laminates are a good choice, but wood veneer is not good near a bathroom where steam can get at it.

Nursery

A baby's bedroom should be planned with the same regard as any aspect of your new child's life – with an eye towards the future. A nursery should also revolve around the child's immediate needs: nursing, feeding, changing. If you succumb to buying charming but impractical baby furniture, try and choose a piece that can be adapted or used elsewhere later on. A good chest of drawers or changing table will usually suffice. Paint the furniture white or a pastel colour, and adorn it with playful handles, knobs and decals (transfers). You can also add a padded, waterproof mat on the top for changing. As for the baby's stuffed animals, toys and knick-knacks, it's best to show them off rather than try and store them neatly away.

Under-fives

Cute as they are, little children can create a storage nightmare. They are an active, inquisitive bunch, and their bedroom will reflect their changing needs. They require masses of equipment,

IKEA

School-age child

Once your child starts school, his or her storage needs will change. A desk with drawers is needed to take the increasing amounts of paperwork that the child needs or wants to keep.

A cork pin-up board also becomes a storage point for favourite pieces of memorabilia, school notices, sports notices, ribbons, badges and those all-important stickers. Rather here than on the fridge or underfoot.

Wardrobe needs are more sophisticated now, with more hanging space needed (see Project 3, Framing up an alcove, on page 34); shoe storage becomes more important, as do bookshelves.

Bunk beds are good in a shared room situation, and many incorporate desks and storage units. Privacy becomes increasingly vital to a child, so provide some storage that can be locked, and give the child a key (keep a spare to cover the inevitable, tragic loss!).

Young childen are avid collectors, so make sure you have a good collection of glass jars, baskets, boxes and tins. A toy box will continue to be invaluable for storage of sports or hobby-related equipment.

Stackable wire baskets for toy storage

FREEDOM

A growing child needs a range of storage accessories

most of which is vital at one stage of growth and redundant at another. In terms of storage, expandable and adjustable units are the most sensible option. They should be safe and durable, and all handles and shelves should be low enough for your child to reach.

In the average toddler's room, you will find nappies, a changing table, a bottom seat, a nappy bucket; a chest of drawers choking with singlets, tops, bottoms, booties, all-in-one suits, a woolly dressing gown, hats; soft toys, mobiles, blocks, a little blackboard; a night light, sheets and blankets; books of all shapes and sizes – the list never ends.

One storage item that is truly vital when young children are around is your basic mothproofed chest or box/boxes. Store as you go along, washing and putting aside clothing or equipment for the next baby – your own, your sister's or your friends'!

Books and toys are the other major storage problem in a young child's room. Putting things out of sight for a while (perhaps in an attractive storage box) is a

good trick with under twos – they think the toys are brand new when re-presented!

The over twos get more sentimentally attached to things as a rule and like familiar things around them. An attractive toy box (make sure the lid cannot drop suddenly and that the box has good ventilation) and a bookshelf that displays books rather than stores them, spine to the forefront, are both practical and decorating assets. Remember that a bed and desk will subsequently take the place of the cot and changing area. Also, bright colours may win out over pastels.

QUICK-FIX PROJECT
Earring racks
Install as many of these racks as your accessories require. Measure inside your cupboard doors to establish the length of each rack. The racks are made of narrow strip steel and are held away from the door at each end by screwing through a rubber doorstop. Drill a hole at the ends of each rack the size of the diameter of the screw for the door stop. Cover each rack with adhesive electrical tape, then screw through the doorstops to the cupboard doors. Scarves can be draped over these racks, and belts can be hung from them after fastening the buckle.

A teenager's room needs to accommodate many different interests

Teenagers

Like it or not, a teenager's bedroom often becomes their favourite habitat, and what once sufficed as a perfectly acceptable chest of drawers is now suddenly 'childish'. Don't despair. In fact, it is probably not such a bad idea to think about renovating a little or investing in some new furniture. A teenager's bedroom often becomes a spare or guest bedroom, eventually, so it might be worth decorating now with that end in mind.

Angular built-ins are a smart idea, and custom-built shelves can house stereo equipment, records, books, magazines and photo albums. Narrow shelves are handy for tapes and books. Divan or sofa beds serve a dual purpose as they can be used for sleeping or sitting – they are ideal, as a teenager's bedroom is also a focal point for visiting friends.

GREEN TIP

Mothproofing
❑ **Place muslin bags, each containing 50 g of ground cloves, cinnamon, black pepper and orris root, among the clothes.**
❑ **Place lavender in gauze sachets between the layers and folds of clothing.**

Storing your clothes

Keeping clothes, shoes, hats or bed linen for long periods of time requires more than simply making sure they are clean.

Store your best linen in blue tissue paper away from light

Fabric needs room to breathe or the fibres will deteriorate. Linen, for example, needs to be kept in a cool place and preferably on slatted shelves to allow the air to circulate around the garment. When hanging your clothes, it is a good idea to separate weekend gear from the less worn outfits. It's also advisable to cover full-sleeved garments with short plastic covers so that the sleeves do not crease.

❑ Do not hang knitted or jersey clothes as they will stretch. Instead, fold them carefully and pack them in a suitcase, drawer or on a shelf; sweaters shouldn't be squashed into drawers as this can also ruin the fibres and may result in permanent creasing. Light-coloured jumpers should be stored in plastic bags to prevent fading. This is also an excellent way to re-use plastic bags.

❑ When folding jumpers, lay the garment face down, fold one side and arm to the middle, fold the arm back down on itself and repeat with the other side. Fold the sweater in two, taking the top down to the bottom with the sleeves inside the fold.

❑ Shirts should be hung on coathangers. If it is necessary to fold and pack them, button the shirt to the top to prevent creasing and to stop the collar from being distorted, lay the shirt face down, turn both sides into the middle, fold in the sleeves (in line with the body) and turn the tail up then fold the bottom up to the collar.

❑ Trousers should be folded along the crease and stored on hangers. To protect against a hanging mark, tape cardboard or wrap a piece of clean cloth around the hanger as padding. Evening gowns should hang inside out to keep them clean. For skirts, sew bias binding

(cloth binding tape) loops on to the inside of waistbands and hang on coathangers; pleats should be tacked in place.

❑ An important factor for proper hanging is that coathangers should fit the garment exactly, spanning the width of the shoulders, and the back should support the neck of the garment. Never use wire hangers.

❑ Leather and suede should be shaken well before being stored so that creases do not set into the garment. They should also be hung in plastic bags.

❑ Furs need to be hung in a well-ventilated and cold place, or stored in sealed plastic bags containing moth repellent.

❑ Precious garments such as bridal and christening gowns, veils or damask table cloths should be completely wrapped in blue tissue paper (to keep moisture out) and stored in a box.

❑ Boots and shoes should be kept on racks so that they are tidy, but also to prevent them from scratching or marking each other. A shoe rack can be easily attached to the inside of a wardrobe. To keep their shape, boots should be filled with tissue paper or newspaper. Galoshes or gumboots can be punctured at the top of the rubber of each boot and hung with string on a hook.

❑ Store bed linen in large plastic bags and keep it on top of a wardrobe, at the foot of a bed in a blanket, or under the bed so it doesn't get too squashed.

❑ Do not store linen in an airing cupboard for long periods as the humidity can damage the fibres.

❑ Accessories can be easily kept in baskets decorated with large bows on shelves in the dressing room. Another idea is to use small decorating hooks, linked by stencilled ribbon and bows, to hang hair accessories, scarves and jewellery – creating a pretty effect in the bedroom.

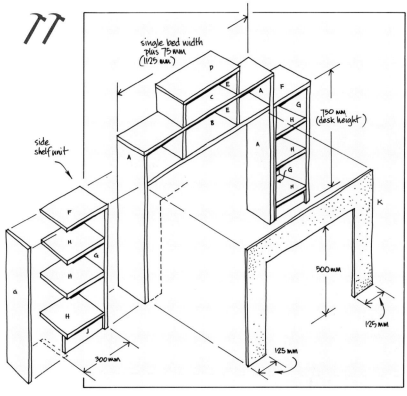

Storage bed-end

Make this fun shelf unit for the end of the bed for your bedtime books and bits and pieces or for toy storage in a child's room.

The size and layout of the shelves and storage recesses can be to any design you choose as long as there is enough room for the bed and pillow to rest against the bed-end.

Our bed-end is for a bed which is accessible from both sides, that is, not placed lengthways against a wall. The two side shelf units are separate so that you can leave these out or change them to suit your particular needs, such as making a larger shelf unit on one side of the bed only, with perhaps a desk space as well.

MATERIALS

ITEM	DIMENSIONS (mm)	QUANTITY
medium-density fibreboard (MDF)	2.4 x 1.2 m x 16 thick 1.8 x 0.9 m x 16 thick	1 sheet 1 sheet
PVA adhesive		
adjustable shelf supports – these come in a variety of types and materials, from brass to plastic		
particle (chip) board screws		
25 mm twisted-shank nails		
panel pins		
all-purpose undercoat and oil-based gloss paint for finishing		

SPECIAL TOOLS
handsaw and power saw
electric drill
hammer and screwdriver
square

TIME
Allow about 8 hours to construct and another two days for the painting (one coat of undercoat and two finishing coats).

STEP BY STEP

1 Follow the cutting diagram for cutting out the panels. Use a guide batten/cleat for the power saw, as described for Project 7 (Deskmate). Start by cutting the main side and top panels (A, B and C) and panel K, which fixes to the end of the bed and acts as a bracing panel. When you have cut each panel, check that the corners are square.

2 Apply adhesive to the edges of the panels and nail together, starting with panels A and K, followed by B and C. At this point you are able to measure for panels E and D. Cut these panels and nail or screw and glue in position, making sure that they are square.

3 The side shelf units are made as separate units which are screwed to each side of the main bed-end. Cut the side panels (G) together with the bottom and top panels (F and H). Drill blind holes into the side panels for the adjustable shelf supports at about 50 mm apart. Now glue and nail these panels together.

Fix the skirting panel (J) in place and make sure the unit is square. It is a good idea to use a piece of offcut timber as a temporary brace at the back until the adhesive is dry and you have finished screwing the panels together. Check-measure and cut the shelf panels (H) ready to fit into place.

4 When you have completed the nailing and gluing, drill-pilot and countersink holes for the screws near each corner. Apply a little adhesive to each screw and screw into place.

5 When complete, use a fine sandpaper to rub down the edges then paint with under-coat. Leave to dry according to the instructions on the paint tin.

Use an oil-based gloss paint for the final coats. This will resist abrasions more easily. Paint on two coats, remembering to sand down with wet and dry sandpaper between coats.

TIP: Nailing provides a handy way to hold panels together while the adhesive sets and you drive the screws. But don't rely on nails alone for strength.

CUTTING SCHEDULE

Item	Dimensions (mm)	Quantity
A	934 x 250	2
B	1093 x 250	1
C	1125 x 250	1
D	625 x 250	1
E	184 x 250	5
F	300 x 250	2
G	734 x 250	4
H	268 x 240	6
J	268 x 100	2
K	dimensions indicated	1

Don't despair when you look at the jumble of tools, gardening equipment, outdoor furniture and all the junk you've accumulated over the years. Ingenuity is the name of the game when it comes to organising outdoor storage areas.

OUTDOOR STORAGE

Storage aids for outdoor areas come in all shapes and forms: rope, nails, screws and hooks; lengths of metal fencing; pieces of timber; metal brackets; door knobs; bricks. You'd be surprised how many things can be useful. Now take stock of your surroundings. The empty overhead and wall space in the garage or carport, the cellar or basement area (see our special Cellar project starting on page 76) and even the nooks and crannies are begging to be used as repositories.

❏ When neither garage nor under-house space is available, a timber or metal garden shed or even a gazebo or a child's play house can provide excellent storage for garden equipment, furniture and tools.

❏ Less elaborate outdoor storage may take the form of a simple cupboard, suitably waterproofed with a sloping roof, built against the wall of the house.

❏ An unsightly water tank or rubbish bin can be stored away and hidden behind slatted timber or latticework panels.

❏ In an outdoor living area, such as a patio or even a conservatory, a long timber seat with a waterproofed, hinged lid could disguise a storage box for garden tools and cushions. Similar seats could be built in a gazebo or as part of a barbecue area.

❏ Cupboards elevated off the ground beside a built-in barbecue can be used to house firewood, extra crockery and a variety of other articles.

❏ Outdoor furniture, a portable barbecue and cushions can be tucked away neatly in an unobtrusive cupboard built against a fence or a wall.

Garage/carport

The garage and, to a lesser extent, the carport have enormous potential for storage, particularly if they have pitched roofs. Think of all that wasted space above the car and how it could be used to store any number of bulky items, from bicycles to boats, from bags to blankets. Often, there will be enough space to add wall shelving or cupboards too. If you do intend to store anything in the carport, consider security and weatherproofing carefully. With suitable insulation, waterproofing and electric wiring you may be able to turn a no-longer-used garage into a home office, a studio, a child's playroom or a fully equipped workroom.

Garden sheds

Where space permits, a garden shed is one of the most practical solutions to outdoor storage and many of the garden sheds today are designed to be aesthetically pleasing as well.

Prefabricated, lock-up sheds are available in a variety of sizes and styles, with hinged or sliding doors. They are easy for the competent

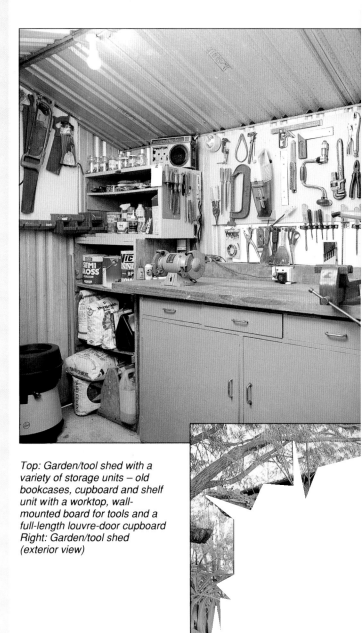

Top: Garden/tool shed with a variety of storage units – old bookcases, cupboard and shelf unit with a worktop, wall-mounted board for tools and a full-length louvre-door cupboard
Right: Garden/tool shed (exterior view)

Make sure your storage areas are well lit for easy location of items.

Clockwise from top: Wooden pegs and tray for easy storage of ski equipment; Timber cupboard with sloping roof for storing firewood and an assortment of outdoor equipment; Metal adjustable shelving; Rubbish bin and hot water cylinder hidden from view by latticework panels

One of life's frustrating moments is to be halfway through a job and unable to find an essential tool: every tool should have its place.

Stack 'N' Store

HANDY STORAGE

❏ Epoxy-coated steel baskets, drawers and cubes provide great storage on or under shelves, either free-standing or on drawer glides in frames with castors.

❏ Any type of storage unit on castors will save time and effort. An old tea trolley tucked under a worktop or bench can be used to wheel things around; timber boxes can have castors attached to make them mobile.

❏ Plastic bins or cardboard boxes in various sizes stacked on shelves can be a neat way of storing any number of items, from sports equipment to seasonal clothes to old books and toys.

❏ Sealed rubbish bins also rate well as storage receptacles. Note, however, that deep bins can be a handicap if you want to fish something out from the bottom.

❏ If there is sufficient space, you could add tall but narrow vertical cupboards for long-handled tools, a lawn mower or sporting gear such as skis and fishing rods. The advantage of having cupboards is that you can lock the doors for safety and security and they will protect goods from dust and moisture. Sliding doors save space.

❏ A timber rack with dowelling pegs or blocks of timber at the top and a wooden tray at the bottom can be made to support skis or any tall sporting equipment.

❏ Cupboards with shelves or drawers placed underneath or above a worktop provide dust-free storage. Old cupboards picked up at a junkyard or retrieved from a kitchen renovation are worth considering for this job.

❏ Safety is always important; any poisonous substances should be locked in an overhead cupboard.

A garden hoserack with real character

home handyperson to install – with a little help.

Most steel-framed sheds come without floors. Ideally, they should be placed on a concrete slab, but specially treated timber decking or pavers can be used. If a shed is raised off the ground, it may be necessary to install some sort of access ramp for large articles such as a lawnmower or a wheelbarrow. Some steel-framed garden sheds come with freestanding shelves and other accessories as optional extras (in this type of shed the walls are usually not strong enough to take heavy weights). Alternatively, you can build your own timber frame within the shed and use this to support shelves on the walls.

Attractively designed rustic timber garden sheds, complete with their own floors, come in kit form in all shapes, sizes and styles – some even with windows and verandas, giving them the look of a mini house.

The more elaborate model with windows may become a workroom, a garden potting centre with worktops, shelves and cupboards – or even a cosy retreat from the daily grind.

Wall storage

While overhead storage has merit when space is at a premium, it is best used for articles which are not needed too often. Wall storage, on the other hand, is more practical for everyday use.

❏ The home handyperson can set up a great work area in an adequately sized garage by putting in a worktop (or an old kitchen table will do) at the far end, with storage space above and on side walls.

❏ Shelves can be wall-mounted, freestanding or hanging. As a rule of thumb, the length of a timber shelf should never be more than 1.2 m for light loads and 800 mm for heavier loads. A good depth for a shelf is around 300 mm.

❏ In a timber-framed garage, simple shallow timber shelves can be built between the studs to hold, for example, jars and boxes of nails, tins of paint or garden products. Make sure that any area where you store tins of paint or any other type of chemical can be locked.

An old bookcase makes a useful freestanding storage unit. Timber shelves can also be hung by rope, which is knotted under each shelf for stability and attached to the rafters or joists with strong hooks. Alternatively, lengths of timber shelving can be placed on bricks or concrete blocks laid on the floor.

❏ Adjustable metal track shelving in different configurations can be fitted to walls. Track shelving can also be used to hold bicycles. Simply set up the tracks as directed for the shelving system, and mount them to wall studs which will support the weight of the bicycle. Pad the brackets to prevent scratching the top tube, and adjust them to the correct height for hanging the bicycle (also see Project 15, Bicycle rack, on page 75).

❏ A pegboard attached to the wall, complete with pegs and hooks for hanging, is an efficient way to hold tools and garden equipment. More upmarket is a metal louvre-panel system which has louvres designed to support various-sized plastic storage containers.

❏ Magnetic bars screwed to the wall are excellent for storage of metal tools.

❏ Hooks can be used to hang anything from a ladder to a bicycle in either a vertical or horizontal position. Two large hooks side by side are ideal for holding garden hoses or lengths of rope.

❏ Never underestimate the humble nail, which can be hammered into the wall or into a piece of board to support a variety of items including tools, garden equipment, and brooms and sporting equipment, such as tennis and squash racquets.

❏ For safety, sharp tools should be kept up high, out of the reach of children. Outlining the shape of each tool with a felt tip pen on the board will make it easy for you to return tools to their correct place after use.

❏ Coat hooks, shelf brackets, door and drawer knobs, and wooden pegs or dowels glued into predrilled holes can all be used for hanging various articles.

Cane basket for storing firewood undercover just outside the back door

Project 15

Sturdy bicycle rack

This bicycle rack is a great idea for storing your bicycle and forms the base frame for overhead storage racks.

About 4.2 m of 75 mm x 38 mm, and 1 m of 75 mm x 25 mm building grade timber is all it takes to build this project.

STEP BY STEP

1 Assemble the bicycle rack by nailing or bolting the brace between the two pairs of uprights. You may need to adjust the dimensions to fit the space and your bicycles. The uprights should overlap the ceiling joists by 75 mm.

2 Cut a 25 mm notch in both ends of the hangers 50-75 mm from the end of the boards. Nail or screw to the end of the rack (see illustration).

3 Slip top of uprights over the ceiling joist and nail or bolt in place.

MATERIALS

ITEM	DIMENSIONS (mm)	QUANTITY
uprights	900 x 75 x 38 (according to available height)	4
brace	600 x 75 x 38 (to match your joists)	1
hangers	450 x 75 x 25	2
flat-head (roundhead) nails	65	
bolts/screws (optional)	6 (minimum diameter)	

SPECIAL TOOLS
electric drill

TIME
3-4 hours

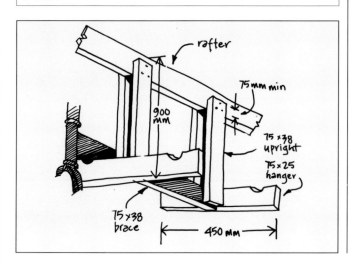

rafter
75 mm min
900 mm
75 x 38 upright
75 x 25 hanger
75 x 38 brace
450 mm

OUTDOORS

Wire plant holder

Overhead storage

Overhead storage can be as simple as using the existing rafters and beams to hold solid items like rolled-up rugs or surfboards, or as sophisticated as installing an electric chain block system to hoist up the family dinghy. When planning overhead storage in a garage, make sure there is adequate headroom – a sensible height for most overhead storage is around 2 m.

❏ Pulley systems. One of the problems of overhead storage is accessibility, which can be a real worry if items are super heavy. This is where pulley systems come into their own. To get cumbersome articles up and out of the way, chain-block or rope-block (block and tackle) systems can be used. Working on a ratchet, the chain block system levers the item up to the required position where it remains stable without having to be secured.

The less sophisticated rope block system works on the pulley principle where the item is winched up and secured by ropes when it is in position. This is easy for the home handyperson to install, and can be used to hold in place anything from a ladder to a canoe.

Awning pulley systems should be used for reasonably light articles only, but can be quite handy if you want to get things up and out of the way without having to use a ladder.

❏ A wooden platform under the joists is another simple method of holding goods. Simply screw or nail shelving to the bottom of the joists and, hey presto, you have a ready-made basket.

❏ Alternatively, screw or nail a large timber shelf to the top of the joists, or suspend a timber platform by ropes or chains from the rafters.

❏ You could also build a tall, solid timber platform on legs for storage at the far end of the garage, high enough off the ground to enable the bonnet of the car to nuzzle in underneath.

❏ Looking for something simpler? A hammock strung across the rafters by hooks is ideal for storing lightweight articles up high.

❏ Firmly anchored hooks are another easy and inexpensive way to hold items overhead. Butchers' hooks hung over the beams and joists will support quite heavy weights. Sturdy plastic-coated hooks can be used to hold bicycles.

Overhead storage rack

And you thought your garage couldn't hold another thing! Just look up – it's nearly that easy to make this suspended storage unit.

The closer this rack is positioned to a side wall, the greater its load-bearing potential for storing all of those bulky extras.

STEP BY STEP

1 Assemble two or more shelf support units, following the instructions given in Project 15 (Bicycle rack, on page 75). The distance between the uprights should not exceed 1200 mm.

2 Attach the shelf support units to ceiling joist as shown. The distance between the vertical support units should not be greater than 900 mm.

3 Nail or bolt 150 mm x 75 mm boards to the brace as shown.

MATERIALS		
ITEM	DIMENSIONS (mm)	QUANTITY
uprights	900 x 75 x 38	12
braces	1000 x 75 x 38	3
boards	1600 x 150 x 25	6
flat-head (roundhead) nails	65	
bolts/screws (optional)	6 diameter	

SPECIAL TOOLS
electric drill

TIME
One day

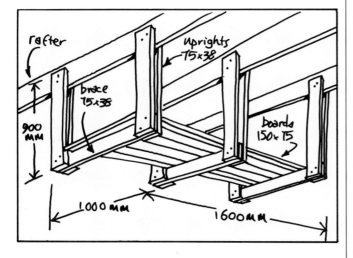

The cellar

Depending on its size, condition and accessibility, a cellar has the potential to hold almost anything.

Older houses often have nonhabitable cellars which have traditionally been used for coal and junk – but with careful thought and planning they can be transformed quite cheaply into efficient and capacious storerooms. Some of the best uses for the cellar are:

❑ Wine and food – the cool conditions suit wine perfectly and will help a freezer to run more efficiently.

❑ Tools and decorating or building materials. If there is room, the cellar may also form a convenient workshop.

❑ Long-term storage of little-used items (such as holiday luggage or seasonal sports equipment).

Practical considerations

A dry, clean, well-ventilated cellar with a solid floor and the walls in good condition can be treated as an extension of the house as far as providing safe storage is concerned. It will be colder than elsewhere indoors, but you might even consider extending the heating system into the cellar if cool storage (such as for wine) is not important. Any suspicion of damp, however, and you are immediately limited as to what you can store in contact with the floor or walls; broadly, only items made of plastics, glass, noncorroding metals such as copper, aluminium and galvanised steel, and preservative-treated timber. Rodents and other pests are another point to watch out for, especially if the floor is bare earth.

The usage will also depend on how easy it is to get into the cellar and whether or not there is enough headroom. Cellars with steep steps and low ceilings are not ideal for manoeuvring heavy, bulky objects in and out of! For the same reason, it makes sense to keep things which you will need frequently near the door. Shallow shelves and wall-mounted hooks, racks and brackets which do not restrict access are best here. Use the hidden depths for storing items that will receive less regular visits.

Surveying the possibilities

To give yourself a clear picture of the potential, work through the points below and check what needs to be done to make the best use of the space.

❑ **Construction:** A cellar may be completely below ground or may be partly above and partly below ground level (semi-basement). The latter type often has a window, exterior hatch or grille, whereas a below-ground cellar will probably have little or no ventilation and natural light. Extra lighting is fairly simple to arrange, but ventilation may be tricky (see page 77).

❑ **Damp:** This is a major consideration since it restricts what can be stored without damage. Test for damp with a meter (available in DIY outlets and builders' merchants) or call in a specialist firm for an estimate. If you test after a spell of dry weather and find no signs of damp, don't assume that this automatically gives the all clear – check again after a period of rain.

Walls can be damp-proofed with chemicals or physically with rendering and waterproof panelling. Both really mean calling in the professionals and can be expensive. There is also some risk that physical treatment may force damp to rise into the room above if there is no damp-proof course (DPC). Bare earth floors are never completely dry, but can be screeded with concrete incorporating a plastic damp-proof membrane (DPM) if there is sufficient headroom to permit the build-up in level (see below).

❑ **Ventilation:** A good airflow is important if the cellar doubles as a workshop, and is essential if you will be using solvents which give off harmful vapours. In any case, ventilation prevents mustiness and helps to control damp and associated problems to some extent. Airbricks can be installed if any of the cellar walls are above ground, whereas an extractor fan (controlled by a humidity detector if desired) can be fitted through a wall or window, but will have to be ducted into a below-ground cellar.

❑ **Cleanliness:** General junk and coal are the usual obstacles. Junk can be sorted and disposed of as required; anything useful can be rehoused in the cellar afterwards in a more orderly way. Removing coal is a bigger task – even if there is very little left, the dust has usually impregnated all the surfaces. The only solution is rubble sacks, a shovel, old clothes, a dust mask, an

industrial vacuum cleaner and time and energy. When you have removed as much as possible, follow up by cleaning and painting.

❑ **Lighting and power:** Storage is only efficient if you can see what you are looking for, and most cellars are lit by a single bulb or nothing at all. Adding fluorescent lighting coupled with white walls will give the best illumination of all areas. If you are in any doubt about what is involved, contact a qualified electrician.

If there is no existing light point to extend from, a separate 20 amp radial circuit from the consumer unit (which is often conveniently sited in the cellar) is the best solution. This can provide power as well, with the lighting being taken via a 5 amp fused connection unit. Another option is to run a 5 amp fused spur from the power circuit in the room above, making sure that by doing so you do not exceed the maximum floor area that the circuit can serve: 100 sq m for ring circuits; 50 sq m for 30 amp radial circuits. The light switch should be close to, but just inside, the door so that it can be turned on without entering the cellar, but cannot inadvertently be switched on from outside and left on unnoticed.

A separate spur will be needed for power outlets. This should be RCD-protected if you intend using power tools.

❑ **Access:** This may be via a trapdoor in the floor, a door under the stairs, or a full-height door (in the case of a semibasement cellar). Access determines what can be stored according to its size, weight and regularity of use, so think about improvements like rehanging a door the other way round to make it

easier to open. Where access is restricted, storage can be arranged around the door so that it can be used like a cupboard.

❑ **Headroom:** Most cellars are below habitable height (2.3 m), but this only means that they must not be used as living areas. If the headroom is less than your own height, the usage is broadly determined by how low you are prepared to stoop. If the floor joists above are exposed, this may make all the difference through being able to stand full-height at intervals between them.

One way to increase headroom may be to excavate the floor, but seek professional advice first to check if this will leave adequate support for the house walls and foundations.

❑ **Size:** Together with headroom, this is the factor that most determines how useful the cellar is – obviously, the bigger the better. If the cellar is 2.4 m or more in width, you can significantly increase the wall storage space by partially dividing it along its length with a racking system.

❑ **Floor:** A smooth, dry floor helps to keep the cellar clean and gives more flexibility as to what can be stored on it. Simple ways to provide hard-standing are to lay paving slabs on a bed of sand around the walls, or to section off these areas with timber and cast strips of concrete. In this way you will not reduce the headroom of the standing area in the middle, and at the same time you will also help to lessen the stooping distance.

❑ **Walls:** These form a large, useful and easily accessible area. Providing the walls are sound, shelves and cupboards can be fixed to them for a

variety of storage. Any timber in contact with the masonry should be well soaked with preservative unless it is pretreated (e.g. Tanalised), and you should leave an air gap behind any cupboard units with a back by mounting them on battens/cleats or simply threading spacers (such as rubber doorstops) on to the mounting screws.

In some cellars the inner 'walls' will be formed by brick pillars supporting the floor above. The gaps between these should not be filled in completely, as they provide essential airflow under the house, although you can still fix things across them.

❑ **Ceiling:** Open joists provide a wealth of hanging space for lightweight items in areas where headroom is not a problem. If the floor above is made of bare boards, panels of fibreboard stapled to the underside will help provide a degree of insulation from noise and dust – especially if the cellar is to double as a workshop. They can also be painted white to reflect light better.

Fitting out

Plan the layout of the cellar with storage systems that suit the items to be kept there, making full use of walls (and open ceilings) as hanging space and providing shelving of different depths. Site storage for long items such as timber opposite the door for easy access and removal.

In an area like this, appearance doesn't matter,

so using what you have to hand or can salvage is the key to successful low-cost storage. Because of this, the following suggestions can only provide useful guidelines.

Remember that any storage is only as efficient as the ability to see what is stored, and this is doubly important in a confined space. Don't make shelves and cupboards too deep, and help to identify small objects by using transparent containers or clear labelling; once an item is hidden by something in front of it, it is effectively 'lost'. Use self-adhesive labels and a marker pen for large unidentifiable boxes and a plastic lettering system (such as Dymo) for smaller containers in regular use.

Saving on the cost of materials by using up offcuts and 'recycled' timber salvaged from builders' skips is ideal, since looks will be relatively unimportant. But make sure that it is free from rot and insect attack.

❏ **Back-to-back racks:** You can add 'wall' space, if the floor width is 2.4 m or more, by erecting a simple floor-to-ceiling stud framework to divide part of the cellar lengthways and provide the storage area of two walls. Use straight, knot-free 50 mm x 50 mm DAR (PAR) softwood – there is no need to line the frame, because cladding means extra work and materials and will cut out light and ventilation, as well as making fixing to the studs more difficult.

In all cases, fix a length of timber to the floor so that you can screw the bottoms of the studs to it. If the frame runs parallel to open ceiling joists, align the floor timber with the closest joist, so you can screw the top of each stud to the side of it. To strengthen this joist, fix bracing between it and the

adjacent joists. Alternatively insert cross-braces between two joists and screw the studs to the braces instead. If the framework runs at right-angles to the joists, screw one stud to each joist. No bracing is necessary. If the ceiling is lined, fix a 50 mm x 50 mm beam to the surface, screwing through it into the joists, and attach the studs to this.

Attach shelf brackets or adjustable shelving supports to both sides of the studs. Aligning the shelves back-to-back like this provides deep shelving that can be reached from both sides; cut notches in the backs of each shelf so that they fit over the studs and span the centre gap. If you can't align the shelves, a batten/cleat along the back of the shelf will prevent things from rolling or being pushed off it. Horizontal battens/cleats can also be screwed part way up the studs to provide bracing and can be fitted with hooks or drilled for dowels to provide hanging space for tools.

❏ **Using alcoves:** These are a ready-made storage area. If there is a fireplace in the room above, the supporting brickwork will probably create three alcoves that can be fitted out with floor-to-ceiling shelves resting on battens/cleats. Doors can be hung on vertical battens/cleats to close off the space, but ensure that there is some ventilation behind them. Louvre doors are especially suitable.

❏ **Using benching:** A horizontal surface fixed around the walls both provides storage in its own right and forms a useful worktop – where space permits, it could even be an unusual venue for an electric train! Suitable dimensions are a height of 900 mm with a depth of 600 mm, and you should use timber at least 20

mm thick, such as old floorboards. Provide support every 900 mm on a 50 mm x 50 mm bearer fixed front to back, with one end set into the brickwork and the front end supported on an upright post.

Shelving above the benching can be of different depths – deep shelves high up for large items and shallow shelves lower down for small ones, so that they restrict the bench space as little as possible. Make sure, however, that the deep shelves are far enough back from the front of the benching to prevent a head-on collision when you bend forwards.

Benching is an obvious place to store tools. Particle (chip) board or MDF panels supported on the back of the benching can be fitted with clips and hooks to store handtools just where they will be needed. By making the boards detachable they can be transferred easily (with help) to other working areas. Use each tool as a template to draw around its outline – to keep it in the right place and to spot what has been borrowed!

Pull-out storage under the benching is best for anything other than large items, since the area at the back is difficult to reach. An old chest of drawers makes an excellent storage unit, but you may need to reinforce the drawer bases with strips of plywood glued underneath, before storing heavy things in them.

Shelving supported on the upright posts can hold plastic storage crates (inserted lengthways front to back). In this case, you will need a second set of uprights, screwed to the wall, to carry cross-bearers for the shelving. Space the shelves to give just sufficient clearance to move the crates in and out so as to keep out dust, especially if

the benching above will be used as a workbench.

Another form of pull-out storage is a wine rack; this should stand on the floor so as to minimise vibration of the contents. Also on the floor, a tea-chest is ideal for storing 'useful' offcuts of timber and the like. Cut a piece of 12 mm plywood to the size of the base and nail this to two timber bearers. Stand the tea-chest on this for additional support and to allow air to circulate beneath it. Castors could be fitted to the bearers to allow it to be pulled out easily.

❏ **Racking:** Long items such as timber are efficiently stored on ladder racks, on which they are accessible from the end and side. Construct the ladder sections from 50 mm x 50 mm DAR (PAR) softwood and secure them to the wall and ceiling. Space the 'rungs' at intervals to suit the sizes of timber that you expect to store (not forgetting sheet materials), and position the racks at 900 mm intervals so as to support timber of this length or over. Anything shorter than that can be kept in the offcut tea-chest. Two stout angle brackets screwed to the front of the uprights will support a ladder – again in a position where it can easily be carried through the doorway. Good access is the key to successful storage.

In emergencies
❏ Ensure that there is a clear route to isolating switches and valves for mains services (electricity, water and gas) and that nothing can be stored in front of them.

GLOSSARY

Batten/cleat: A sawn strip of wood used to cover joints or to provide support.

Brick veneer: Building method with a structural timber frame and a veneer of brick on the exterior.

Built-in: Made or incorporated as an integral part, e.g. a built-in cupboard.

Cabinet timber: Fine-quality, dressed (planed) furniture-grade timber.

Cooktop (hob): A separate flat surface in the kitchen containing hotplates or burners.

Custom-built, custom-made: Made to the specifications of an individual customer.

DAR (PAR): Dressed all round (planed all round). Timber that is smooth, as in planed.

Decoupage: Process of decorating a surface with shapes or illustrations cut from paper, card, etc.

DIY: Do-it-yourself.

DPC: Damp-proof course.

DPM: Damp-proof membrane.

Dressed (planed) timber: Timber which has a smooth surface usually done by using a plane or machine tool.

Ergonomics: The study of the relationship between workers and their work environment; rules for designing to the correct dimensions for effective and comfortable use.

Faux: False or fake.

Flat-head (roundhead) nail: Large general-purpose nail (20-150 mm).

Freestanding: Not attached to or supported by another object.

Grout: The (compressible) filler between tiles.

Hardboard: A manufactured pulp board, used as an underlay for resilient tiling or panelling.

Hardwood: Wood from broad-leaved flowering trees such as eucalypt, oak, beech and ash.

Header: The timber member over a small opening.

Housing: A shallow trench in timber to provide lateral restraint in a joint.

Jack stud: A short stud.

Jamb: The rebated frame into which a door closes.

Joist: A horizontal framing member to which are fixed floorings or ceilings.

Knockdown furniture: Easily dismantled and assembled (kitset).

Lining: Interior wall covering.

Lintel: A structural support member over openings.

Make good: Return to original, or finish off.

MDF board: Medium-density fibreboard – a high-quality manufactured pulp board.

Modular system: Add-on system made up of standardised units of furniture (each unit is designed to be added to, or used as, part of an arrangement of similar units).

Mortar: Cement, lime and sand mixture for adhering bricks and tiles.

Nogging: Short framing members joining the broad face of studs.

Nosing: Front edge of a step.

Painted finish: Paint is applied to a surface to protect it and to either create contrast or to help an item blend with existing surroundings. Common techniques used include dragging, rag rolling, sponging and stippling.

Particle (chip) board: A manufactured wood sheet made of wood chips and adhesive.

Pier: Masonry column supporting structure above.

Plate: The topmost and bottommost members of a frame, to which studs are joined.

Plinth: The rectangular slab or block that forms the lowest part of the base of a column, pedestal or pier; a flat block on either side of a door frame, where the architrave meets the skirting; a flat base on which a structure or piece of equipment is placed.

Polyurethane: A hard yet resilient coating commonly used for wear areas.

PVA adhesive: Polyvinyl acetate adhesive.

Renovation: Update from the original.

Restoration: Process whereby the style of a piece is retained and its original finish restored.

Revamping: Process whereby the original form of an item is retained but its finish and character is altered.

Reveal: Timber extension of a window frame to the interior.

Screed: Levelling of materials using a straight edge.

Scribed joint: A butt joint where one surface matches the profile of the adjoining one.

Sealer: A coating to provide a suitable surface for final coatings.

Secret nailing: Method of nail fixing panelling so that nails are not visible.

Softwood: The open-grained wood of any coniferous trees such as pine and cedar.

Stencilling: Process of applying a design to a surface consisting of a thin sheet of plastic, metal, cardboard, etc, in which the design has been cut so that ink or paint can be applied through the cutout area onto the surface.

Stopping compound: A filler or putty for filling blemishes in timbers.

Stud: The vertical member of a timber frame.

Trenching: See Housing.

Trompe l'oeil finish: A painted or decorated effect which gives an illusion of reality.

CONVERTING MEASUREMENTS

Although most people have some working knowledge of metrics, many cannot visualise the actual size of a metric measurement. Hopefully the following chart will help.

LENGTHS

1 mm approx $^3/_{64}$ inch

10 mm approx $^3/_8$ inch (a mortar joint, thickness of the average little finger)

25 mm approx 1 inch (everyone knows what an inch is!)

230 mm approx 9 inches (1 brick)

820 mm approx 32 inches (an average door width)

2400 mm approx 8 feet (10 bonded bricks, or minimum ceiling height)

1 m approx 39 inches

1.8 m approx 6 feet (a tall male)

2.04 m - just under 7 feet (the height of the average door)

3 m approx 10 feet

VOLUMES

1 litre approx 1.8 pints (a carton of milk)

4.5 litres approx 1 gallon (a large paint tin)

AREA

1 sq m approx 1 sq yd

9.3 sq m approx 1 building square – 100 sq ft

INDEX

ACKNOWLEDGMENTS

Many people helped in the course of producing this book. Apologies to any individuals or companies not specifically mentioned. Special thanks go to Geoff Phillips for assistance with locations; Graheme McIntosh, Interior Design consultant; Gieffe, Luxury Kitchens and Bathrooms; Laura Ashley, IKEA; FREEDOM; and Country Form for supplying photographs.

The Publisher also wishes to thank the following: Paul Frank, Architect, and Judy Green Interiors for assistance with locations; Clarke and Walker Pty Limited, Mitre 10, for kindly supplying tools (pp. 6-7); Hafele Australia; Sterling Mail Order; Australian Flora Designs; In Residence, Flossoms and Blue and White Drycleaners (for props, p. 70); and Janet Niven's Antiques (for throw rugs, p.20).